DANGEROUS PASSAGE

A Maritime History of the Torres Strait

IAN BURNET

DANGEROUS PASSAGE

Contents

	Dedication	viii
	Foreword	xi
	Prologue	xv
1	The Islands of the Torres Strait	1
2	Luis Vas de Torres finds the Torres Strait, October 1606	8
3	The Dutch find the Torres Strait, 1606 and 1623	21
4	Abel Tasman searches for a passage through the Torres Strait, 1644	30
5	James Cook finds a passage through the Torres Strait, 1770	39
6	Timor and Kupang (Coepang)	57
7	Mutiny - William Bligh and the Bounty, 1789	63
8	The Search for the Bounty Mutineers, 1791	80
9	Escape from Port Jackson, 1791	92
10	William Bligh's Second Chance, 1791	105
11	Shah Hormuzeer and Headhunters in the Torres Strait, 1793	120
12	Mathew Flinders sails to Port Jackson, 1795	128
13	Mathew Flinders circumnavigates New Holland, 1803	139

14	Mathew Flinders's third voyage through the Torres Strait, 1803.	152
15	Phillip Parker King completes the mapping of Australia, 1818	163
16	West to East - The Voyage of the Zenobia, 1823	171
17	The Charles Eaton and Head-hunters in the Torres Strait, 1834	176
18	The French are stranded in the Torres Strait, 1840	184
19	Hydrographic Surveys in the Torres Strait, 1837 – 1850	194
20	The Rescue of Barbara Thompson, 1849	201
21	The Founding of Port Albany and Somerset, 1864	208
22	Pearls and Priests, 1860-1914	216
23	Thursday Island and the Torres Strait Pilots, 1877	221
Epilogue		229
Bibliography		232

Copyright © 2024 by Ian Burnet

All rights reserved. No part of this book may be reproduced in any manner whatsoever without written permission except in the case of brief quotations embodied in critical articles and reviews.

Published in Australia in 2024 by Alfred Street Press

I would like to thank my wife Yusra Zahari and my daughters Miranda and Melissa who have supported all my writing ventures.
Thanks to Jeffrey Mellefont for providing the cover image.
Thanks to Sarah Hamylton for providing a map of the Torres Strait
My thanks as well to all those who work at the State Library of New South Wales for their assistance.

The cover image is from a painting of the *Rattlesnake* by Oswald Brierly (detail)

It has been said that the ship influenced our history more than any other thing, and even more important were the mariners who manned her. Their greatest challenge was the passage via the Torres Strait, even more so than the rounding of Cape Horn. Either the tortuous Inner Route along the Great Barrier Reef or the Outer Route up through the reef-strewn Coral Sea with a dangerous crossing of the Barrier to follow.

Conway's History of the Ship

Foreword

In 1888, a three-masted Barque was chartered to sail from Sydney to Mauritius to collect a cargo of sugar. A northern voyage outside the Great Barrier Reef and through the Torres Strait allowed the captain to pay homage to his boyhood heroes, the great navigators and explorers like Luis Vas de Torres, Abel Janzoon Tasman and Captain James Cook. This is what he wrote of the voyage:

> All of a sudden, all the deep-lying sense of exploring ventures in the Pacific surged to the surface of my being. Almost without reflection I sat down and wrote to my owners suggesting that instead of the usual southern route, I should take the ship by way of Torres Strait. I ought to have received a severe rap on the knuckles, if only for wasting their time in such an unheard of proposition. I must say I awaited the reply with some trepidation. It came in due course, but instead of beginning with the chiding words, "We fail to understand," etc., etc., it simply called my attention in the first paragraph to the fact that "there would be an additional insurance premium to pay for that route," and so on, and so on. And it ended like this: Upon the whole, however, we have no objection to your taking the ship through Torres Strait if you are certain that the season is not too far advanced to endanger the success of your passage by the calms which, as you know, prevail at times in the Arafura Sea.
>
> I read, and in my heart I felt compunctious. The season was somewhat advanced. I had not been scrupulously honest in my

argumentation. Perhaps it was because I never expected it to be effective. And here it was all left to my responsibility. My letter must have struck a lucky day in Messrs. H. Simpson and Sons' offices — a romantic day. I won't pretend that I regret my lapse from strict honesty, for what would the memory of my sea life have been for me if it had not included a passage through Torres Strait, in its fullest extent, from the mouth of the great Fly River right on along the track of the early navigators? The season being advanced, I insisted on leaving Sydney during a heavy south-east gale. Both the pilot and the tug-master were scandalised by my obstinacy, and they hastened to leave me to my own devices while still inside Sydney Heads. The fierce south-easter caught me up on its wings, and no later than the ninth day I was outside the entrance of Torres Strait, named after the undaunted and reticent Spaniard who, in the seventeenth century, first sailed that way without knowing where he was, without suspecting he had New Guinea on one side of him and the whole solid Australian continent on the other — he thought he was passing through an archipelago — the strait whose existence for a century and a half had been doubted, argued about, squabbled over by geographers, and even denied by the disreputable but skilful navigator, Abel Tasman, who thought it was a large bay, and whose true contours were first laid down on the map by James Cook, the navigator without fear and without reproach, the greatest in achievement and character of the later seamen fathers of militant geography.

If the dead haunt the scenes of their earthly exploits, then I must have been attended benevolently by those three shades — the inflexible Spaniard of such lofty spirit that in his report he disdains to say a single word about the appalling hardships and dangers of his passage; the pig-headed Hollander who, having made up his mind that there was no passage there, missed the truth by only fifty miles or so; and the great Englishman, a son of the soil, a great commander and a great professional seaman, who solved that question among many others and left no unsolved problems of the Pacific behind him. Great shades! All friends of my youth! It was not without a certain emotion that, commanding very likely the first, and certainly the last, merchant ship that carried a cargo that way — from Sydney to Mauritius — I put her head at daybreak for Bligh's Entrance, and packed on her every bit of canvas she could carry. Windswept, sunlit empty waters were all around me, half-veiled by a brilliant haze. The first thing that caught my eye upon the play of green white-capped waves was a black speck marking conveniently the end of a low sandbank. It looked like the wreck of some small vessel. I altered the course slightly in order to pass close, with the hope of being able to read the letters on her stern. They were already faded. Her name was *Honolulu*. The name of the port I could not make out. The story of her life is known, by now to God alone, and the winds must have drifted long ago around her remains a quiet grave of the very sand on which she had died. Thirty-six hours afterwards, of which about nine were spent at anchor, approaching the other end of the strait, I sighted a gaunt, grey wreck of a big American ship lying high and dry on the southernmost of the Warrior Reefs. She had been there for years. I had heard of her. She was legendary. She loomed up, a sinister and enormous memento mori raised by the refraction of this serene afternoon above the far-away line of the horizon drawn under the sinking sun. And thus I passed out of Torres Strait before the dusk settled on its waters. Just as a clear sun sank ahead of my ship I took a bearing of a little island for a fresh departure, an insignificant crumb of dark earth, lonely, like an advanced sentinel of that mass of broken land and water, to watch the approaches from the side of the Arafura Sea. But to me it was a hallowed spot, for I knew that the *Endeavour* had been hove-to off it in the year 1770 for her captain, whose name was James Cook, to go ashore for half an hour. What he could possibly want to do

I cannot imagine. Perhaps only to be alone with, his thoughts for a moment. The dangers and the triumphs of exploration and discovery were over for that voyage. All that remained to do was to go home, and perhaps his great and equable soul, tempered in the incessant perils of a long exploration, wanted to commune with itself at the end of its task. It may be that on this dry crumb of the earth's crust which I was setting by compass he had tasted a moment of perfect peace. I could depict to myself the famous seaman navigator, a lonely figure in a three-cornered hat and square-skirted laced coat, pacing to and fro slowly on the rocky shore, while in the ship's boat, lying off on her oars, the coxswain kept his eyes open for the slightest sign of the captain's hand.

Thus, the sea has been for me a hallowed ground, thanks to those books of travel and discovery which have peopled it with unforgettable shades of the masters in the calling which, in a humble way, was to be mine, too; men great in their endeavour and in hard-won successes of militant geography; men who went forth each according to his fights and with varied motives, laudable or sinful, but each bearing in his breast a spark of the sacred fire.

Joseph Conrad, Captain of the *Otago*, in *Last Essays*

Prologue

The reef-strewn passage between the Australian mainland and Papua New Guinea remains the most hazardous of all the major straits in the world. Although it is 270 kilometres long and only 150 kilometres wide, its tropical waters contain over 274 islands and 580 coral reefs. These waters are full of potential hazards separated by narrow and often dangerous channels.

The Torres Strait lies at the boundary between two ocean basins, the Coral Sea and the Arafura Sea, with sea levels to the east typically higher than those to the west, leading to strong and unpredictable currents. Depending on the time of the year, massive amounts of water, which are being transferred between the Pacific and Indian Oceans, surge through the Torres Strait, creating hazards for shipping. Regional currents flow from the Coral Sea into the Arafura Sea from April to December and then from the Arafura Sea into the Coral Sea from January to March. As an area of confluence between two ocean systems, the tidal patterns are complex. Tidal heights can change up to 3 metres, stream rates can exceed 7 knots, and gradients can be very short. For example, it can be high tide at one end of the Prince of Wales Channel and 40 minutes later, low tide at the other end of the channel, only 20 kilometres away.

The Torres Strait Islanders know these waters well because voyaging and trade were part of their lifetime and their livelihood, but the early European explorers like Luis Vas de Torres and James Cook were forced to find their own route through the Strait without any previous maps.

Trade inevitably followed human settlement, and soon after the arrival of the first Europeans to settle on Australian soil in 1788, shipmasters were looking for economical routes to and from the new colony. Supplies would have to come from the north, and Torres Strait was a logical shortcut for ships sailing to or from Port Jackson and the Asian ports of India, Singapore, and Batavia (Jakarta). The safest route was to sail around the northern coast of New Guinea. However, finding a passage through a gap in the Great Barrier Reef and then across the Torres Strait would save around six weeks on a voyage from the new British penal colony at Sydney Cove (New South Wales) to British ports in India, which were to be the main source of supplies. To enter the Torres Strait from the east, they had to either navigate the tortuous Inner Route inside the Great Barrier Reef or follow the Outer Route through the reef-strewn Coral Sea and then make a dangerous crossing through a gap in the Great Barrier Reef and into the Torres Strait. To enter the Torres Strait from the west was made difficult by the easterly winds and currents that prevailed for most of the year. For those ships that could navigate these hazards and attempt to cross the Torres Strait, there was also a culture of headhunting on the islands, which led to the deaths of some of the early European sailors.

Hundreds of 18th and 19th-century European shipwrecks offer a testament to the dangers of navigating this region in sailing vessels. The Australian Register of Shipwrecks lists as many as 200 shipwrecks occurring in the Torres Strait and its vicinity between the years 1800 and 1900, with the loss of as many as 333 lives. As you would expect, the exact details of many of these shipwrecks are incomplete.

It was not until the completion of detailed hydrographic surveys of the Torres Strait undertaken by the British Admiralty, the advent of steamships and the introduction of Torres Strait Pilots that a relatively safe passage could be made through the Strait for commercial shipping. The Prince of Wales Channel is now the main route for vessels passing through the Strait but is limited to ships with no more than 12.2 metres of draught. A Torres Strait pilot is required on board to ensure both a safe passage and the protection of the environment, as there have been examples of ships running aground and destroying the coral.

This book will follow the history of the Torres Strait Islanders, the first sailing voyages by Europeans who tried to make this dangerous passage, how they discovered various navigable routes, and the numerous shipwrecks that occurred in the process. It was the voyages of these early navigators, such as Torres, Cook, Bligh, Flinders, and the British naval hydrographers, such as King, Wickham, Blackwood, Yule and Stanley, who contributed to the charting of the Torres Strait and ultimately its use as a major shipping route.

Readers should be advised that this history will include stories of murder, mayhem, mutiny, disastrous shipwrecks, desperate voyages of survival in open boats, headhunting and hurricanes.

I

The Islands of the Torres Strait

Torres Strait Islanders are a saltwater people, proud of their separate and distinct culture, rich in language, music and dance, strong in dignity and community solidarity, and exuberant in spirit.

Michael C Quinnell, from Queensland Museum's Awakening: Stories from the Torres Strait exhibition, 2011.

To understand the formation of the Torres Strait, we must look back to the end of the last Ice Age. Before this time, the Torres Strait was a plain studded by a series of low hills that connected the Australian and New Guinean parts of the Australian Continent. About 20,000 years ago, the earth began to warm at the end of the last Ice Age, and the global ice sheets started to melt. As a result, sea levels rose some 100 metres, and the coastline that once lay near the edge of the Australian Continental Shelf began moving inland.

The presence of sea-rolled pumice buried on Badu Island indicates that the sea arrived in the Torres Strait around 8000 years ago and reached its present configuration about 4000 years ago. As the land bridge was flooded, corals flourished in its warm, shallow waters, and their tiny skeletons became the framework upon which successive generations grew as the water level continued to rise. All this resulted in an area bounded by the Arafura Sea on the west and the Coral Sea on the east, which contains the islands, coral reefs, and coral cays of the Torres Strait and the Great Barrier Reef.

The Australian aborigines were the first humans to reach Australia during a period when lower sea levels exposed large areas of the Sunda Shelf in Southeast Asia and the Sahul Shelf of the Australian continent. It is not possible that the Aborigines could have walked to Australia, but the ocean crossings were much narrower then than they are today, and simple canoes or rafts would have allowed them to cross.

The Torres Strait Islanders were originally of Aboriginal descent in the western islands, of Papuan descent in the northern islands, and of Melanesian descent in the eastern islands. At the time of European contact, the population was thought to be between four and five thousand people. Each community exploited the resources of the surrounding reefs, islets, sandbanks and a much larger region, including the two mainlands, through trade. Many of the Islanders still survive on subsistence farming of cassava, taro, bananas, yam and coconuts, as well as hunting turtles, dugongs and different varieties of fish.

The Islanders have a strong seafaring and trading tradition, and each island community amounted to a sovereign unit bound only to the other communities by the need for trade. This inter-island trade knotted Islander communities together in reciprocal ties necessary for life. The staples of the eastern islands were coconuts, yams, sweet potatoes, bananas, taro and sugar cane. The central and western islands had turtles and dugongs. The northern islands near Papua had large logs that came floating down the Fly River and were required to build their sailing canoes.

The five Island groups are the Inner Islands (Keriri, Muralug, Ngurupai, Waibene) traditionally known as Kaurareg. The lower Western Islands (Badu, Mabuiag, Mua or Moa) are traditionally known as Maluilgal. The top Western Islands (Boigu, Dauan, Saibai) are traditionally known as Saibailgal. The Central Islands (Iama, Masig, Poruma, Warraber) are traditionally known as Kulkalgal and the Eastern or Murray Islands (Mer, Ugar, Erub) traditionally known as Meriam Le.

The Kaurareg are seafaring Aboriginal people and are acknowledged as the traditional owners of the Inner Islands of the Torres Strait (or the Prince of Wales Island group). Before European contact, Kaurareg used outrigger canoes and other watercraft to navigate their homelands while maintaining close cultural, marriage, and trading ties with Aboriginal groups in the northern part of Cape York.

The lower Western Islands, such as Badu, consist of low hills covered with granite boulders, lightly wooded and with open grasslands. Less fertile than the Murray Islands, the soil still permits the cultivation of sweet potatoes, bananas, and yams. The people of Badu continue to practice traditional hunting, fishing, gardening and trade as they have done for thousands of years. Art is a pivotal part of their way of life, and common themes reflect their intrinsic relationship with the land, sea and sky.

The upper Western Islands of Boigu and Saibai are only nine kilometres south of the coast of Papua New Guinea. These islands are subject to seasonal flooding. In 1947, Saibai Island was devastated by a combination of wet season rain and king tides, which submerged the main village under metres of water. Concerns increased about the island's ability to support future generations, and some of its people decided to move to Bamaga on the Cape York Peninsula. The islands are still at risk of flooding due to rising sea levels. For this reason, a sea wall has been constructed to protect the remaining village on the island as part of a $40 million program of coastal protection works constructed across five islands in the region. The island of Dauan is different because its granite hills stand high above sea level as it is the last part of the Great Dividing Range that runs up the east coast of Australia. Because of the proximity to the Papuan coast, an amendment to the Torres Strait Treaty between Australia and Papua New Guinea allows free movement along this coast so the traditional inhabitants of both countries can trade and share food as one people.

The sandy and isolated cays of the Central Islands were semi-permanently inhabited by groups using large double-outrigger sailing canoes, which could only be constructed from large tree trunks washed down the Fly River in Papua New Guinea. These large outriggers provided marine vessels that could remain at sea for long periods and hold large sea animals such as dugongs and turtles.

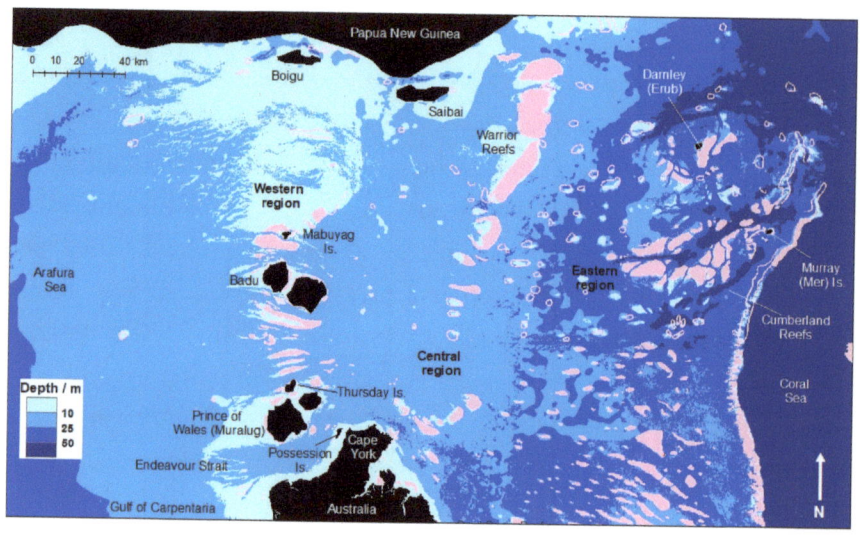

Torres Strait Map
Courtesy of Sarah Hamylton

The eastern Murray Islands (Mer, Dauar and Waier) are the richest in the Torres Strait because of their fertile volcanic soil, which supports tropical vegetation, including coconuts, bananas and varieties of yams. The surrounding sea supports a variety of marine life, and being close to the Great Barrier Reef, the water contains many sharks and rays. The lack of seagrass means that dugongs are scarce, although turtles are plentiful, and Maizab Kaur (Bramble Cay) at the very northern end of the Great Barrier Reef is one of the most important nesting sites for turtles in the Torres Strait. Archaeological evidence suggests that people of Melanesian descent inhabited these eastern islands from 2500 to 3500 years ago.

Melanesian society, as in Papua New Guinea, was intensely xenophobic. Strangers were generally held in deep suspicion, so much so that anyone who travelled far from home went at the risk of their life. Islander society was undoubtedly dominated by violence as many of the Islanders were widely feared as head-hunters, and the legends of the islands abound with stories of raids, ambushes, massacres and captured heads.

The eastern boundary of the Torres Strait is the Great Barrier Reef, which extends more than 2000 kilometres along the east coast of Australia from Queensland's Hervey Bay to the coast of Papua New Guinea. Long white lines of breakers form and reform endlessly as the Pacific Ocean rolls in upon the reef's seaward edge, while its inner rim shelters long corridors of quiet water. Deep, narrow channels of dark blue water between the coral formations of the Great Barrier Reef allowed early sailing ships to make a hazardous crossing from the Coral Sea into the Torres Strait.

The linguistic diversity in the Torres Strait tends to follow this same geographical separation. Saibai is the language of the western islands that extend north to Papua New Guinea and is related to the Paman languages of northern Australia. Kala Lagaw Ya is the traditional language of the Central islands. The Miriam Mer language is related to the Kiwai language of coastal Papua that is spoken in the Murray Islands (Mer, Waier and Dauar), Darnley Island (Erub) and Stephens Island (Ugar). From the 1850s onwards, the South Sea Islanders who came to the Torres Strait brought a pidgin English that had developed in the Pacific region during the last century. This became a common language for the different language groups that worked in the pearling industry, and 'Torres Strait Broken' is now used by most of the island groups. However, English is the main administrative language and is the language of instruction in the Torres Strait schools.

Island life swings around the axis of the two great seasons of the year. For most of the year, the winds come across the Pacific from the southeast. Until in the rainy season the winds come from the northwest and the Indonesian Archipelago. Islanders learn from an early age to read the signs of the ebb and flow of tides and currents, of rips and whirlpools, and wind and rain patterns. They know when to prepare the land before the rains, when to plant, and when to harvest. They know when the turtle-mating season is and when the trevally, mackerel, queenfish and barracuda are plentiful. The Torres Strait harbours a rich and highly diverse marine ecosystem. It is a major habitat of the sea mammal dugong (dhangal) and is also a sanctuary for six of the seven species of sea turtles. The Torres Strait Fisheries Act controls the hunting of these species, supports their sustainability, and the rights of traditional fishing and hunting.

The Islander's world came to span the migration pattern of the Torres Strait Pigeon. These white birds thrive on the red aril, known as mace, that surrounds the nutmeg seed growing in the Indonesian Spice Islands and then fly southward to feed on the red plums of the wongai trees of the Torres Strait, then towards the end of the southeast season they move to lay their eggs among the mangroves on the east coast of the Cape York Peninsula. The Torres Strait Pigeon joins Indonesia and Australia together, and every islander knows the legend that if you eat a wongai fruit, you will become like a bird and always fly back to the islands.

Badu has become a centre for Islander art, especially because of the fame of Alick Tipoti. As a custodian and cultural ambassador for the Torres Strait or Zenadth Kes, his desire to keep his cultural practices alive is at the heart of all his work. His works include interpretations of traditional masks worn by the Islanders, where each mask has a different meaning and was worn only by men in sacred ritual ceremonies. His art also uses linocuts to depict traditional knowledge, often with the canoe as a key symbolic vessel that connected the ancestors to the moon and stars used for navigation. Dance is also an important cultural marker for the people of the Torres Strait and has become the most visible and exciting expression of Islander culture.

Torres Strait Islander people view land and sea as a continuum, and as seafaring people, they are skilled navigators, fishers, and hunters. The sea is fundamental to their identity, livelihood and economic prosperity. They maintain cultural exchange practices, ceremonial feasting and rites of passage, while small-boat fisheries are a source of food and revenue for the Islanders. From time immemorial, their life has revolved around the seasons, which have been marked by the sightings of specific animals and birds, changes in vegetation, tides, weather, and the movement of the constellations.

The colony of Queensland annexed the Torres Strait region in 1872 and 1879; after the Federation in 1901, it became part of Australia. Today, around 4,000 people live on 17 island communities, of which Thursday Island has the biggest population. However, as greater employment opportunities exist on the Australian mainland, many Torres Strait Islanders now live and work in Queensland.

Torres Strait Flag
Bernard Namok

Designed by Bernard Namok, the Torres Strait flag won a local competition held by the Islands Coordinating Council and was recognised by the Aboriginal and Torres Strait Islander Commission in 1992. The green panels at the top and the bottom of the flag symbolise the land to the north and south, while the blue panel in the centre represents the waters of the Torres Strait. The thin black stripes between the green and blue panels signify the Torres Strait Islanders themselves. The white five-pointed star at the centre of the flag represents the five major island groups, and the white dhari is a ceremonial dance headdress that symbolises the Torres Strait Island people.

However, the Islanders' world was to change forever when, in the 1600s, Europeans, both Spanish, Dutch, and English, arrived seeking to find a navigable route from the Pacific or Indian Oceans through the Torres Strait.

2

Luis Vas de Torres finds the Torres Strait, October 1606

> We were for 34 days among the shoals which run out to sea southwards for 50 leagues, in 4 or 5 fathoms of water.
>
> The Relacion of Don Diego de Prado, Madrid, 1615

Luis Vas de Torres and Don Diego de Prado were awakened on the morning of 11 June 1606 with the news that their Flagship *San Pedro and San Paul*, with their commander Pedro Ferdinand de Queirós had departed the bay at Austrialia del Espirito Santo (Vanuatu) during the night. As described by Luis Vaz de Torres in his account to the King of Spain:

> From within this bay and from the most sheltered part of it, the *Capitana* departed at one hour past midnight without any notice given to us and without making any signal. This happened on the 11th of June 1606.

Torres waited at Espiritu Santo for fifteen days for his commander and the Flagship to return. With the failure of Queirós to return, Don Diego de Prado was now the expedition chief with Torres as his captain. Together, they opened the sailing orders given to them in case of separation from the Flagship and, according to Prado:

> Torres summoned the council and produced a closed and sealed paper and said it was from the Viceroy of Peru. It said that in case the ships should separate, they should make every effort to go to 20 degrees of south latitude to see if there was land in that region, and if not, they should proceed to the city of Manila.

The Victoria crossing the Pacific Ocean
Abraham Ortelius 1592, The National Library of Australia

The concept of Terra Australis as necessary to keep the Earth happily spinning on its axis and to maintain the balance of the Earth's distribution of land above and below the equator dates back to the ancient Greeks. A 1592 map by Abraham Ortelius shows Magellan's ship *Victoria* crossing the Pacific and depicts the land south of the Strait of Magellan as stretching across the entire Southern Ocean. The land is named *Terra Australis Magellica Non Dum Detecta* or 'The South Land of Magellan Not Yet Detected'. It is also interesting that this map shows a strait separating *Terra Australis* from New Guinea, which is depicted as an island, although Ortelius noted that this was not proven.

Bounded by four continents, the Pacific Ocean is Earth's largest feature and was unknown to Europeans until the Spanish explorer Vasco Nuñez de Balboa sighted it in 1513 from a peak in Panama and then completed crossing the Isthmus of Panama to wade into its waters. The Treaty of Tordesillas (1494) and the Treaty of Saragossa (1529) granted Spain rights to all lands discovered in the western hemisphere up to the Moluccas (the Indonesian Spice Islands). This meant the Spanish believed they 'owned' the Pacific Ocean and all its undiscovered lands and islands, including the as-yet-undiscovered *Terra Australis.*

Spain's major exploratory expeditions of the Pacific, launched from its colonial bases on the west coast of South America, were motivated by a combination of Christian fervour and gold fever. Pedro Sarmiento de Gamboa, a Spanish soldier and navigator, arrived in Peru in the 1550s and became the leading authority on Inca legends and history. He theorised that such a highly developed and rich society was not indigenous to South America and had come from a land to the west, possibly from the undiscovered Terra Australis. Others speculated that perhaps the Incas had brought their gold with them from Ophir, the biblical region where the stones are described as being made of gold, and from where King Solomon had received cargoes of gold to build his temple in Jerusalem. If this was the case, then Terra Australis, Ophir, and all the gold must be located out there, somewhere in the vastness of the Pacific Ocean!

After the voyages of the Spanish explorers Sarmiento and Mendana to what they optimistically named the Solomon Islands, Pedro Ferdinand de Queirós returned to Spain to seek financial support for another expedition. Probably knowing the difficulties, he first petitioned Pope Clement VIII to support the continuation of the Spanish discoveries in the Pacific. Queirós told the Pope of the 'infinity of souls' waiting to be saved for Christianity and the lands and riches waiting to be discovered, lands that were already designated as being in the Spanish half of the world. The concept was magnificent – vast dominions to be discovered and added to the Spanish empire, millions of souls to be saved and brought into the Catholic faith and more riches of gold and silver.

With the Pontiff's blessing, Queirós then approached King Philip III of Spain, who, after two years of the claimant's petitions, agreed to sponsor a third voyage of discovery. The King's orders declared that he took particular inclination and pleasure in the prospect that the discovery would bring the holy faith to those remote peoples, and he signed a letter ordering the Peruvian viceroy to give all necessary aid to Queirós. The Viceroy provided three ships: the flagship San Pedro and San Paul, commanded by Queirós; a second vessel named San Pedrico, commanded by Luis Vaz de Torres; and the launch named Los Tres Reyes, commanded by Pedro Bernal Cermeño, all with 159 soldiers, sailors and some Franciscan friars onboard.

The small fleet left the Port of Callao in December 1605 to search for Terra Australis Incognita in the vast vastness of the Pacific Ocean, and Queirós described their departure:

> The sails were set, and the men on their knees prayed for a good voyage ... All the artillery, muskets and arquebuses were fired off. The ships passed near the royal ships, which were saluting with their cannon, with many people on their decks and galleries.

On April 30, 1606, they reached not the Solomon Islands but the islands of the New Hebrides (Vanuatu). Arriving from the north, the Queirós fleet entered a large bay backed by the mountains of Vanuatu, which certainly appeared large enough to be the gateway to a continent.

Queirós took possession of this land for Spain and named it in honour of King Phillip III's Austrian royal house, declaring:

> I take possession ... of all this region of the south as far as the Pole, which from this time shall be called Austrialia del Espiritu Santo, with all its dependencies and belongings; and this forever, and so as right exists, in the name of the King, Don Philip III.

Queirós named the bay after St. Phillip and St. James; its port was to be called Vera Cruz, and the city to be erected nearby was named New Jerusalem, with its gates and church built of marble. Such a grand declaration had to be followed by a grand act. Queirós elevated his officers to be Knights of the Holy Ghost and other senior crew members to be magistrates of New Jerusalem. However, there was no gold, and Don Diego de Prado, a genuine Knight of Calatrava and the most senior member after Queirós thought this was nonsense and later wrote:

> It was all wind, both walls and foundations, for he sought to cover up thus what he had promised on the way and was mistaken ... I said to him before his friends ... God has given you Indians, not only two but thousands as in the islands ... and now this land which you call the great Austrialia of the Holy Ghost. We have only found the black devils with poisoned arrows. What has become of the riches? We quite understand that all your affairs are imaginary and as such have gone off with the wind.

Unhappy with Qeuirós, Prado transferred himself from the flagship to the *San Pedrico*. Those on board the flagship were obviously of the same opinion because, as Queirós lay ill in his cabin and too weak to assert his authority, his crew decided they would leave the bay and return to Peru. Torres waited at Espiritu Santo for fifteen days for his commander and the Flagship to return. With the failure of Queirós to return, Don Diego de Prado was now the expedition chief, with Torres as his captain. Together, they opened the sailing orders given to them in case of separation from the Flagship, which said that in case the ships should separate, they should make every effort to go to 20 degrees of south latitude to see if there was land in that region. If not, they should proceed to the city of Manila.

The galleon *San Pedrico* and the tender *Los Tres Reyes* then sailed southwest in a last attempt to locate Terra Australis. Facing difficult weather and an equally difficult crew, Torres gave up the search at 21 degrees south, an estimated 300 kilometres from the mainland of Australia. After turning north, they reached the Louisade Archipelago off the east coast of New Guinea. Here, the *San Pedrico* was forced to follow the south coast, hoping that the 1592 map of Abraham Ortelius was correct and that it was, in fact, an island. In 1528, the Spaniard Alvaro de Saavedra, commanding the Santiago, attempted to sail from the Spice Islands of Eastern Indonesia back across the Pacific and charted the north coast of New Guinea. However, no one had mapped the south coast of New Guinea, and if it was an embayment, then Torres was sailing into a trap because the dominant easterly winds would have made it almost impossible for him to sail back. This was a considerable risk, but we don't know how much thought was given to this decision and as described by Torres:

> From hence, I stood back to the N.W. to 11½° S. latitude: there we fell in with the beginning of New Guinea, the coast of which runs W. by N. and E. by S. I could not weather the east point, so I coasted along to the westward on the south side.

The vessels continued along the south coast of New Guinea for the next two months, and several landfalls were made to replenish the ships' food and water. According to Prado:

> These Indians have an abundance of yams, which are roots they sow like potatoes, and they are extremely good cooked in a

pot with meat; plenty of sweet canes of which they make sugar; sweet basils as big as a man, which serve them for food; and wild amaranths, green, yellow and red.

At some point, they collected some native children to take back to Spain as evidence of their voyage and as described by Prado:

> I selected fourteen boys and girls from six to ten years old and sent them on board; the rest, I let go free, and they ran up a hill like goats. We found a girl of about fourteen years old with the most lovely face and eyes that could be imagined; her whole body painted with stripes like a Milanese corselet, and her private parts covered with a red apron reaching to her knee, made of the bark of trees. There were disputes about who was to take her to the ship, so considering that some might fall away with her and offend God, I delivered her up to a good old woman of her own people; she thanked me greatly in her manner and wanted to go off with the rest, which she did forthwith.

Prado writes later that these children were baptised when they reached Manila, perhaps as some sort of justification for their kidnapping. The vessels continued sailing a course along the south coast of New Guinea until they reached the Gulf of Papua, near the mouth of the Fly River, where their vessels were blocked by the coast and shallow water. Hence, they were forced to turn south and encountered a multitude of reefs and shoals in 3 to 5 fathoms of water for the next 34 days. Fortunately, the *San Pedrico* found a southwest passage and, for more than a week, ran between the reefs until they reached what they called Isla de los Perros (Island of the Dogs), which Brett Hilder has identified as Zagai Island. Here, the expedition did not hesitate in taking young women on board, and Prado is more explicit about their purpose:

> When searching the island, we met with a number of women who were very well-disposed, and two men guarded them. One

of the men climbed up a high tree and left a bow and arrows on the ground. Many signs were made to him, but he would not come down. We shot at him with the arrows, and he caught them all in his hand. It was an extraordinary thing. At last, they let off an arquebuse at him and he fell lifeless. We selected three of the youngest women and put them on board for the service of the crew. The inhabitants of these islands live on turtle flesh and it is in 10° latitude.

From here, the expedition turned west towards what became known as Turnagain Island but could not find a way through the reefs and had to turn back. Prado's narrative describes how they weathered an intense tropical storm:

> We tried again to go to the great land, but the shoals were so large that we could not get across. On the next night there came such a great wind and tempest while we were anchored that it seemed as if all the elements had conspired against us; so that at midnight we all made confession and prepared to die; of the two cables with which we were anchored one broke, but in commending ourselves very truly to Jesus, Maria and Joseph, Jesus was pleased to have mercy on us. So great was the water and sand that entered along the bowsprit that the upper deck of the ship was half blocked up. At dawn, the storm ceased, and the sea became as calm as if there had never been anything.

Torres found that the currents in the Strait were so strong that, at times, it was necessary to have two men at the helm to keep the ship's head against the stream. The last thing the captain of any vessel wants to do is run aground at high tide, so Torres and his crew came up with a different method of sailing. The vessels would wait until the tide started to recede, then let their ship drift with the current, which led them to the deepest channels. Once the tide appeared to be rising again, they would anchor and wait for the next receding tide to make further progress. Prado describes this method as coming from a divine revelation:

> Seeing that we could not get clear of these shoals, we took counsel as to what was to be done and decided not to weigh anchor until ebb water and go with the foresail only to direct the ship because the stream would carry the ships through the trough of the water, and then to anchor at the flow of the tide. The opinion was as if it had come from heaven, for in this way, we secured the ships and saved our lives.

They were amongst reefs and shoals until they reached the channel immediately north of Cape York, which James Cook subsequently named the Endeavour Strait. For many years, it was assumed that Torres took a route closer to the New Guinea coast to navigate the strait that now bears his name. However, in 1980, Captain Brett Hilder demonstrated from the descriptions by Prado that Torres took a southerly route through the strait past Marulag (Prince of Wales Island) and would have sighted the mainland of Australia.

Torres became the first European to navigate the strait that bears his name and, by doing so, proved that New Guinea was an island. The galleon *San Pedrico* and the tender *Los Tres Reyes* had persevered for 34 days among the shoals of the Torres Strait in 4 or 5 fathoms of water and invented a new method of sailing before they could reach the deeper water of the Endeavour Strait and exited into the Arafura Sea. As Torres reported sailing as far south as 11°, they would have sailed through the Endeavour Strait, and the large island he reported seeing on the southern side would have been the *Terra Australis* they had been sent to discover. Having cleared the Torres Strait in October 1606, the expedition then followed the Papuan coast to the northwest until somewhere near the island of Batanta where they encountered a local trading vessel and a Portuguese speaker who told them they were only five days sail from the island of Bachan in the North Moluccas, where there was a Jesuit priest. Prado wrote in his chronicle:

> It is impossible to exaggerate the pleasure we all felt at such good news, and certainly, for us, he was like an angel, for we had already given ourselves up for lost... we thought it was so until this man told us where we were. We gave thanks to God.

In response to the Dutch capture of the Portuguese forts in Ambon, Tidore and Banda the Spanish sent a war fleet from Manila to capture Fort Gammalamma on the island of Ternate from the Sultan of Ternate in 1606. On reaching this island, the Torres expedition anchored off Fort Gammalamma and remained there for three months to recover their health. Before Torres left for Manila, the commander of the Spanish fort requested he leave the *Los Tres Reyes* and twenty men to reinforce the fort from an expected Dutch attack.

To their great relief, Torres, Prado and the *San Pedrico* eventually reached Manila in May 1607. Torres sent his report to the Spanish King the following month, stating that he would report in person as soon as the colonial authorities assisted his return voyage to Spain. This letter dated Manila, July 12, 1607, and relating to their voyage through the Torres Strait, was received in Spain on June 22, 1608. A report from the Spanish Council of State to the King advises that this recent discovery should be kept secret, and the letter, which is in the Biblioteca Nacional Madrid reads:

> I fell in with the beginning of New Guinea, the coast of which trends from east to west, a quarter north-west and south-east. I could not go up it by the east side, so I went coasting to the west and on the south side it is all the land of New Guinea. It is peopled by Indians, who are not very white, and naked, although their middles are well covered with the bark of trees, after the manner of cloth, much coloured and painted. They fight with javelins and bucklers, and some stone clubs, with many gaudy feathers about them. There are along the coast other inhabited islands ... Having run 300 leagues of coast, as

has been said, and decreased our latitude by two degrees and a half, so that we remained in nine degrees, at this point there begins a bank of from three fathoms to nine, which stretches along the coast from seven degrees and a half and the extremity of it is five degrees. We could not go forward on account of the numerous shoals and strong currents that are there throughout, so we had to go out by the southwest course by the said deep channel until eleven degrees, and the shoal is lower there. There were some very large islands and more were seen towards the south ...

Dated in Manila, 12 July 1607. Luis Vas de Torres

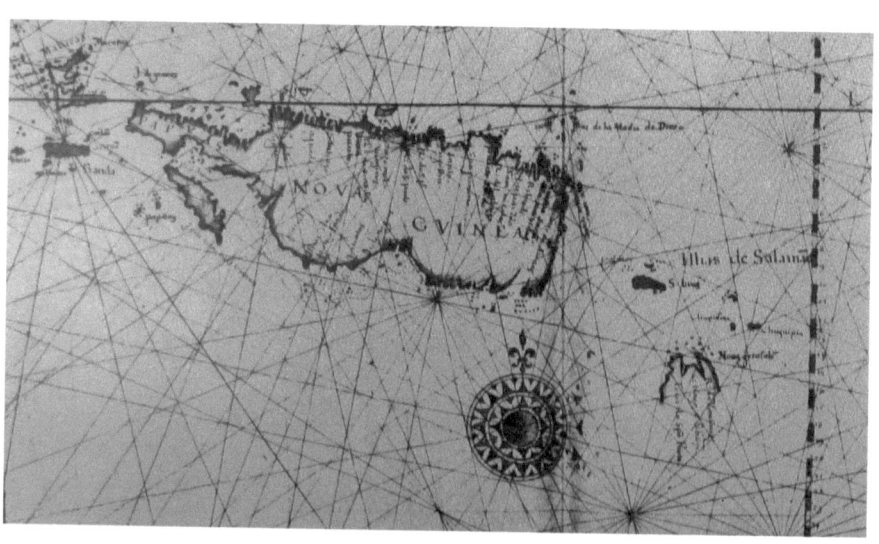

Map of New Guinea from the Duchess du Barry Atlas 1615-23
Bibliotheque national de France

There were five charts included in this report, of which four charts of harbours still exist, but the most important chart, showing their voyage through the Strait, has disappeared into the Spanish archives. However, a map found in the *Duchess du Barry Atlas* must have been derived from the Torres voyage as it shows both the north and south coast of New Guinea annotated in Spanish as well as the Solomon Islands and the recently discovered *Austrialia del Espiritu Santo* or Vanuatu. It also shows the large shallow bank of reefs, rocks and islands that forced Torres to sail southwest towards the Endeavour Strait but does not show any of the many large islands that appeared more on the southern side as described by Torres, which would have been part of Australia.

The next we hear from Torres is in a letter complaining that the Manila administration would not expedite his voyage home:

> Being in the city of Manila at the end of a year and a half of navigation and discovery among the lands and seas in the unknown southern part, and seeing that in this Royal City of Manila, they have not hitherto thought fit to give me dispatch for completing the voyage Your Majesty commanded ... I have thought proper to send a person to give an account to Your Majesty.

Unfortunately, this is the last we hear from Luis Vas de Torres, and it is unknown if he ever left Manila or survived the voyage back to Mexico and Spain. Diego de Prado could travel on a Chinese vessel from Manila to Macao and then on a Portuguese ship via Malacca and Goa. From Goa, he sent a letter and maps showing their discovery of the south coast of New Guinea to the Spanish King dated 24 December 1613, which reads:

> I send to his Majesty, via the Viceroy of the Indies, the map of the discovery which was effected by Luis Vas de Torres, Captain of the Almiranta of de Queirós, who followed the instructions given by the Conde de Monterrey which was the discovery of the island called by us La Magna Margarita, which has 680 leagues of coast. Your Majesty will see by the said Map that all which Pedro Fernandez de Queirós, the liar and

impostor, discovered were some rocks and small islands, for his crew mutinied in the bay of the island of *Espiritu Santo*.

Of course, La Magna Margarita would be the land of Papua New Guinea, which Torres and Prado had proved to be an island. The map of their voyage through the Torres Strait, as referred to by Torres and mentioned by Prado at the end of his Relación Sumaria, has not yet been discovered in the Spanish archives.

Don Diego de Prado eventually returned to Spain, where he became a monk at St Basil the Great of Madrid. In 1615, he published his narrative of their voyage from Lima until they reached Manila. This thirty-two-page manuscript appeared in England some 200 years later in the collections of Sir Thomas Phillips during the 19th century. At the sale of some of Phillips' manuscripts in 1919, it was purchased by booksellers Henry Stevens, Son and Stiles, who sold them to the English collector Sir Leicester Harmsworth. The State Library of New South Wales in Australia then acquired it from Harmsworth's collection in 1932. In 1980, the Queensland master mariner Captain Brett Hilder used Prado's narrative to follow their voyage through the Torres Strait in his book 'The Voyage of Torres'.

The voyages of discovery by Sarmiento, Mendaña, Queirós and Torres were Spain's last major attempts to explore the South Pacific Ocean. The expectations of vast dominions to be added to the Spanish empire, the millions of souls to be saved and brought into the Catholic faith, and the discovery of riches in gold and silver did not happen, and a government severely strapped for funds had to cut its losses.

1606 was a busy year in Australian history because, in March of that year, a Dutch vessel landed on the Cape York Peninsula and, on its return voyage, sailed past the western entrance to the Torres Strait.

3

The Dutch find the Torres Strait, 1606 and 1623

> We were according to the chart we had with us and the estimation of the skippers and steersmen, no more than 2 miles from Nova Guinea, so that the space between us and Nueva Guinea seems to be a bight to which on account of its shallows we have given the name of *drooge bocht* (shallow bight) in the new chart.
>
> Jan Carstensz, Captain of the *Pera*, 1623

In 1603, the Dutch East India Company sent a war fleet to the East Indies with orders to capture the Portuguese forts on the Spice Islands of Ambon, Tidore and Banda. Twelve heavily armed warships commanded by Admiral Steven van der Hagen sailed in 1603, including the Duyfken (The Little Dove), which was built to act as a scout vessel and to carry messages between vessels of the fleet. The sturdy little *Duyfken* measured 20 metres in length, her rig comprised three masts and six sails, and as many as 20 crew members were packed into this tiny vessel. The *Duyfken* had been given a special mission, and at the end of 1605, she sailed from Bantam in Java with orders to explore New

Guinea under the command of Willem Jansz and its chief merchant, Jan van Roosenjin. There are no surviving ship logs of this voyage in the VOC files, but the English East India Company records a report from their trade representative in Bantam, Captain John Saris:

> The eighteenth (November 1605) here departed a small pinnasse of the Flemings, for the discovery of the island called Nova Ginnea, which, as it is said, affordeth great store of Gold.

The *Duyfken* first sailed to the Banda Islands and the newly established Dutch trading post there before setting off on its historic voyage along the south coast of New Guinea. After calling at the islands of Kai and Aru, Willem Jansz followed a southeasterly course before reaching the estuary of the Digul River. From here, they sailed along False Cape before turning south and east to become the first European explorers to reach Australia when, in March 1606, they sighted the low-lying west coast of the Cape York Peninsula. Climbing the rigging to get a better view of what was beyond the low sweep of the coast, they could not see any mountains bearing gold or silver in the interior, although there were columns of smoke indicating that the land was inhabited.

Their first landing was at a river they described as Rivier met het Busch (river with bush). Today, a sandy spit covers part of the entrance into the Pennefather River, which then broadens into a large estuary that extends a few kilometres inland. The *Duyfken* would have needed fresh water and firewood for the cook's stove, so they lowered the ship's boat and rowed ashore. They carried arms in case of trouble, but the local aborigines were astounded to see a boat this size, filled with strange white people, and probably kept out of sight.

From here, the Duyfken headed south and entered a wide bay that they called Vliege or Fly Bay after these most ubiquitous Australian insects. Further down the coast, they charted *Dubbel Rivier* or Double River at the confluence of the Watson and Archer Rivers. They sent their longboat upriver, where they obviously caught some good fish, as they named it *Rivier Vis* or Fish River. Finally, the *Duyfken* reached a point they marked on their chart as *Cabo Keerweer* or Cape Turnabout.

On their voyage down the coast and during his landings ashore, the Chief Merchant, Jan van Roosenjin, had only seen a dry, desolate land inhabited by primitive people. The aborigines were not wearing cloaks of silk or jewellery of gold or silver, there were no mountains that might contain silver or gold, and there were no spice trees, nothing that could be of value to Dutch merchants. Here at Cape Turnabout, the crew of the Duyfken decided they had seen enough and turned around. Willem Jansz assumed that this coast was a southern extension of Papua New Guinea; on his map, it is named Nova Guinea.

Returning northwards, the *Duyfken* passed an island that is marked on their chart as *Hooghe Eylandt* (High Island, Prince of Wales Island, Maralug), which marks the western entrance into the Endeavour Strait and then continued further north until they found their course barred by shoals which they named *Vuijle Bancken* (Vile Banks). Turning west, they rounded False Cape before turning away from the coast towards the Aru and Kai islands and then returning to Banda to report on their voyage. Captain John Saris in Bantam heard of the return of the *Duyfken* from a local trader who had arrived from Banda, as he reported:

> The fifteenth of June (1607) here arrived Nockhoda Tingall a Cling man from Banda in a Java Junke, laden with mace and nutmegs which he sold to the Guzerats. He told me that the Flemmings Pinnasse, which went upon the discovery for Nova Ginny, was returned to Banda, having found the island but were constrained to return, finding no good to be done there.

Willem Jansz and the brave little *Duyfken* will always be remembered for their historic voyage to Cape York, the first European landing on the Australian continent in March 1606, and the observation of the western entrance to the Torres Strait.

News of Luis Vas de Torres's arrival at Fort Gammalamma on the island of Ternate and that he had sailed along the southern coast of New Guinea must have filtered through to the Dutch on the other side of the island at Fort Malayo.

In 1617, the Dutch East India Company appointed Hessel Gerritsz as their cartographer, and it was his task to provide charts for all ships of the VOC that sailed from the Dutch Republic. The discoveries of the *Dufyken* now appeared on the 1622 map of the Pacific Ocean (Mar del Sur) by Hessel Gerritsz, and the text written next to the Cape York Peninsula recognises the possibility that this is the discovery of a new land, separate and different from the island of New Guinea as a notation reads:

> These parts were sailed into with the yacht of Torres about Nueva Guinea on 10 degrees westward through many islands and dry banks and over 2, 3, 4 fathoms for full 40 days. Presuming Nueva Guinea not to stretch over the 10 degrees south – if this were the case – then the land from 9 to 14 degrees must be separate and different from the other Nueva Guinea.

Separate and different from the other Nueva Guinea means it must be part of Australia. This map, held in the Bibliothèque Nationale de France is hugely significant because it is the first time any actual part of the Australian continent appears on a world map.

In 1623, a year after this map was published, the VOC sent a second expedition to the Gulf of Carpentaria, the *Pera* under the command of Jan Carstenz and the *Arnhem* under the command of Dirck Meliszoon. We are fortunate that the *Pera* log still exists and describes their voyage in complete detail. The ships sailed from Ambon with orders to extend Willem Jansz's earlier survey and hopefully find the entrance to the Strait discovered by Torres.

The Carstenz expedition followed the same route along the south coast of Nova Guinea as the *Duyfken*. Here, the central mountains of Papua reach almost 5000 metres above sea level and are always covered in clouds. However, at a certain time during the voyage, the clouds suddenly cleared, and the crew of the *Pera* had this amazing sight, for above them, they could see mountain peaks covered in snow, which Jan Carstenz marked on his chart and described in his log as a *sneeberg* (snow mountain):

> We were about one mijl distance from the low-lying land in 5 or 6 fathoms, when at a distance of about 10 mijlen by estimation into the interior we saw a very high mountain-range in many places white with snow, which we thought a very singular sight, being so near the equator.

No doubt these observations drew much hilarity in the inns and households of Batavia and Carstenz would have been accused of suffering from 'tropic fever' for whoever heard of snow at the equator. But he was later proved correct, for there is a tropical glacier on top of the highest mountain in Papua at 4884 metres, and the Dutch named it Carstenz Top in his honour.

The reference on the Hessel Gerritsz map of 1622 to 'the yacht of Quiros' indicates that the Dutch had come into information that revealed the voyage of Torres along the southern part of New Guinea and the Carstenz expedition had been instructed to find the entrance to this Strait and follow its eastern extension as far as possible. When they reached the shallow bight marked on the Duyfken Map, the longboat was despatched from the *Pera* with the mate, twelve men and provisions for four days to explore the open water. This was the most important part of the expedition because the discovery of this passage could provide a route from the Indian Ocean into the Pacific Ocean. However, they were well north of Endeavour Strait and the longboat returned after just one day with the news that they had found only shoals, mudbanks and shallow water where the Strait might be:

> We were here in 9° 6' S, Lat., about 125 miles east of Aru, and according to the chart we had with us and the estimation of the skippers and steersmen, no more than 2 miles from Nova

Guinea, so that the space between us and Nueva Guinea seems to be a bight to which on account of its shallows we have given the name of *drooge bocht* (shallow bight) in the new chart.

The expedition continued south and reached the low-lying coastline of the Cape York Peninsula, which the *Duyfken* discovered. Deciding not to stop at the first landing of the *Duyfken* they continued further south past Cape Keerwer.

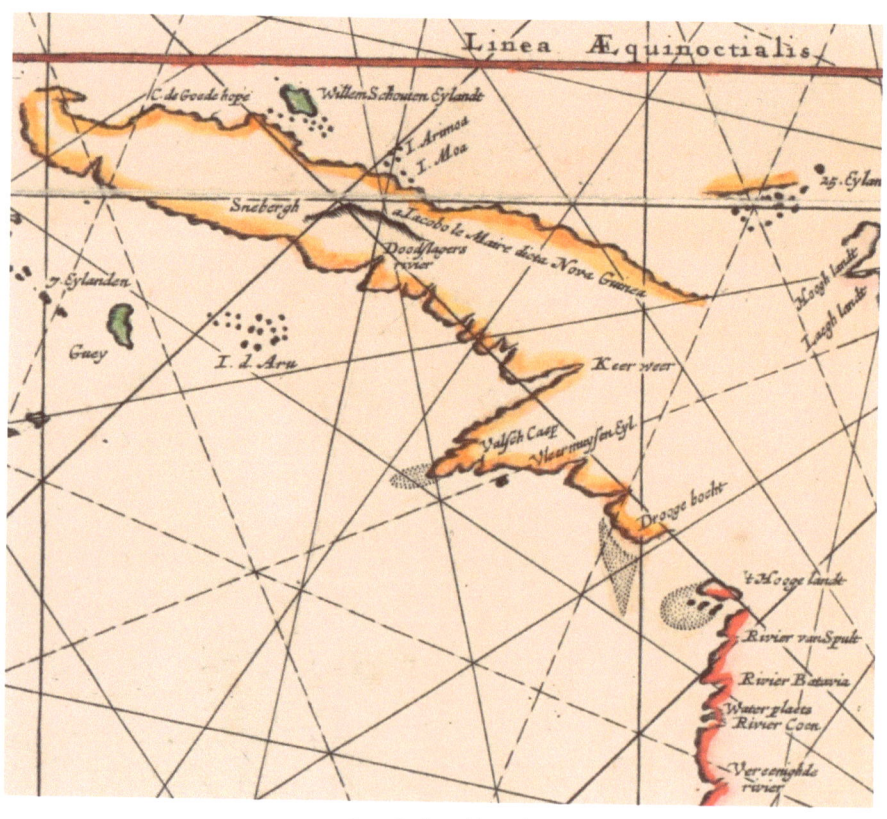

Oost Indien (detail)
Arnold Colom

The expedition reached the southernmost part of the Gulf of Carpentaria and a river they named the Staten River, after the States-General of the United Provinces. Accompanied by some crew members, Carstenz went inland and observed that the land 'was flooded in several places and in appearance was similar to the Waterland in Holland, so that he concluded that further inland there are large waterways and lakes'. Having found no stone they could use to mark the end of their voyage, the crew of the *Pera* nailed a wooden tablet to a tree, which read that 'On the 24 April 1623 there arrived here two yachts dispatched by their High Mightiness the States-General. We have accordingly named the aforesaid river, the Staten River in the new chart. (17 degrees 8 minutes south)'.

There had been problems with the vessel *Arnhem*, initially with its rudder, then it nearly foundered in heavy seas and later collided with the *Pera*, which Jan Carstenz complained was due to poor seamanship. At some point on their return voyage up the coast, the *Arnhem* abruptly decided to leave the expedition and take a more direct route back to Ambon, as described by Carstenz:

> In order to wait for the *Arnhem* which was only a howitzer's shot astern of us; in the evening, having come to anchor, we hung out a lantern, that the *Arnhem* might keep clear of us in dropping anchor, but this proved to be useless, for on purpose and with malice forethought she sailed away from us against her instructions and our resolution, and seems to have set her course for Aru (to have a good time of it there), but we shall learn in time whether she has managed to reach it.

After the ships separated, the more westerly course of the *Arnhem* resulted in charting what was named Arnhem Land. The *Pera* continued on its northerly course along Cape York, and on the afternoon of 11 May, Carstenz describes sailing past a large river, where he believed the men of the *Duyfken* went up with a boat in 1606 and where one of them was killed by the spears of the aborigines. He also describes how, in landing here, the Aborigines had been more hostile than those they had encountered to the south:

> The Aboriginals seem much more acquainted with muskets, of which they would seem to have experienced the fatal effect when in 1606 the men of the *Duyfken* made a landing here ... I went ashore myself with the skipper, and found upwards of 200 savages standing on the beach, making a violent noise, threatening to throw their arrows at us, and evidently full of suspicion; for, though we threw out to them pieces of iron and other things, they refused to come to parley, and used every possible means to wound one of our men and get him into their power; we were accordingly compelled to frighten them by firing one or two shots at them, by which one of the blacks was hit in the breast.

The *Pera* continued sailing north and reached what would become known as the Endeavour Strait and a river that they named Rivier van Speult (Jardine River). Here, was a navigable western entrance into the Torres Strait, which could perhaps lead the Dutch into the Pacific Ocean, but by this time, the second expedition had seen enough of Cape York. On his return, Jan Carstenz wrote a report that would influence any further Dutch exploration of Australia:

> The land between 13 and 17 degrees is an arid and poor tract without any fruit tree or anything else useful to man; it is low and monotonous without mountain or high wooded in some places with bush and little oily trees; there is little fresh water and what there is can only be collected from pits specially dug; there are also no points or inlets ... In general, the men are barbarians all much alike in build and features, pitch black and entirely naked, with a knotted net on their head and neck for keeping their food in and what they mainly live on (as far as we have seen) were certain roots which they dig out from the earth ... we saw many

and different huts made of dry hay; also a great number of dogs, herons and waterfowl and other wild fowl and also very excellent fish which can easily be caught in a net; they have no knowledge at all of gold, silver, tin, iron, lead and copper; even nutmegs, cloves and pepper which had been shown to them several times on the voyage and made no impression on them. In our judgement this is the most arid and barren region that could be found anywhere on earth.

Jan Carstenz, Captain of the *Pera*, May 1623

For the Dutch East India Company, there seemed to be no justification for further exploring the southern reaches of what they had named Nueva Guinea, and it would be 21 years before another Dutch expedition entered the Gulf of Carpentaria.

4

Abel Tasman searches for a passage through the Torres Strait, 1644

> In sailing along the coast, you will have all the bays and inlets you may meet with diligently examined, and keep a sharp lookout for the discovery of channels or openings that might afford a passage into the South Sea.
>
> Anthony van Diemen, January, 1644

Anthony van Diemen was formally sworn in as Governor-General of the Dutch East India Company in Batavia on the first day of January 1636. The following nine years that he served were extremely important for the Company's commercial success. He devoted much of his energy to expanding the power of the VOC throughout Asia since, under his rule, they defeated the Portuguese both in Sri Lanka and Malaya and extended the Dutch trading empire from India to Japan. Accordingly, Anthony van Diemen could now turn his attention to further exploration of the lands to the south of the East Indies.

By this time, the Dutch had assembled an intriguing puzzle of the land or lands to the south of Java. The west coast of Cape York had been mapped, but was this part of Nova Guinea or a part of a Southland? Parts of the west coast of Western Australia had been charted and named Eendrachtlandt. The south coast of Western Australia had been charted between Cape Leeuwin and the Nuyts Archipelago off South Australia and named Nuytsland. Were these discoveries a series of islands, or were they joined together into a single continent? Anthony van Diemen had maintained his interest in the concept of Terra Australis and asked Francois Visscher, the VOC chief geographer and cartographer in Batavia, to draw up plans for a voyage of discovery to the southern ocean. Visscher's proposal dated 22 January 1642 stated:

> An expedition should leave Batavia about the middle of August in order to take advantage of the long summer days in the southern latitudes. The ships should proceed to Mauritius, where water, firewood, and other necessities could be taken on, thence south to the parallels of 51 to 54 degrees latitude and then steer east till they reach the longitude of the east end of Nova Guinea or of the Solomon Islands. They should then turn north and return to Batavia by the north coast of these islands.

It seems the Dutch now believed in a Southland, which was the seemingly worthless land described by Jan Carstenz, and an Eastland, which could contain the imagined wealth of Terra Australis and which some believed had been encountered by Queirós. If there were riches to be found in the known but undiscovered Terra Australis, then Anthony van Diemen wanted to be the man to do it. His idea to organise a major voyage of discovery towards the Pacific and its contribution to geographical knowledge would become his most enduring legacy.

Abel Tasman was named commander of this new expedition and could choose from among the most experienced seafarers in the Batavia roadstead to man his two vessels: the flagship *Heemskerck* with 60 crew and the armed transport ship *Zeehaen* with 50 crew. François Visscher, who had planned the voyage, was appointed pilot-major and commander of the *Zeehaen*. Isaac Gilsemans was appointed chief merchant and sailed on that same vessel. The vessels sailed west from Java, south from Mauritius and then east across the southern ocean, an ocean where no men had sailed before and with no knowledge of what hazards may lay before them. You can imagine the trepidation that Tasman and the crew felt as the cold winds and huge waves of the 'Roaring Forties' pushed them forward into completely uncharted seas. Their long nights would have been full of nightmares of being suddenly dashed against unknown rocky shores before being plunged into freezing waters to die a cold and lonely death. In the late afternoon of 24 November 1642, they sighted distant mountains and, thankfully, still in daylight. These mountains, clothed with dark forest, were on Tasmania's west coast near Macquarie Harbour and Tasman's journal records:

> This land being the first land we have met with in the South Sea and as it has not yet been known to any European we called it Anthony Van Diemen's Land, in honour of the Governor-General, our illustrious master, who sent us out to make this discovery. The islands round about, as many as were known to us, we have named after the Honourable Councillors of India.

Tasman left Van Diemen's Land without personally stepping ashore, meeting its people, or knowing if it was an island. It is interesting to speculate that if he had decided to sail north along the east coast of Australia, then the whole continent would have become known as New Holland, and history would have been very different. However, he had his orders, which were to continue sailing east. On 7 January 1643, the fleet headed out into the South Pacific and passed New Zealand, Tonga and Fiji before returning along the north coast of New Guinea.

It was a remarkable voyage as only six men had been lost to illness and another four killed by natives in New Zealand. Tasman had managed to circumnavigate Australia without ever seeing the mainland, but he had discovered new lands at Van Diemen's Land and New

Zealand. Even though this voyage had not yielded any immediate material advantage to the Company, van Diemen was mostly pleased with its outcome.

There were questions that still needed to be answered. Was the Southland a complex of islands or one vast continent? Was there a passage still undiscovered by the Dutch between New Guinea and the Southland that would lead to the Pacific Ocean? Was the Gulf of Carpentaria the entrance to a strait stretching towards the south or east and providing another route to the Pacific Ocean? The following year, Tasman and Visscher were given command of a second expedition with three smaller ships, the *Limmen*, *Zeemeeuw*, and *de Bracq*, to explore Australia's northern coastline. Their instructions from the Council of the Indies were to explore the unknown coasts of the Southland together with the channels and islands that were presumably lying between them:

> In sailing along the coast you will have all the bays and inlets you may meet with, diligently examined, and keep a sharp lookout for the discovery of channels or openings that might afford a passage into the South Sea, since we may surmise that such passage must be looked for to the northward than to the southward.
>
> In case you should discover channels leading to the South Sea, or should find the Southland to consist of islands, you will endeavour to pass through or between the same, diligently observing the mouths and outlets, and then returning again through the same passage in order to proceed with your discovery along the northside.
>
> Signed, Antonio van Diemen, Cornelis van de Lijn, Joan Maetsuijker, Justus Schouten and Salomon Sweers. This 29th of January 1644

On 30 January 1644, the expedition left Batavia for the Banda Islands with three small vessels, thought more able to explore the passages they hoped to find. Tasman and Visscher sailed on the 120-ton yacht *Limmen* with a crew of forty-five sailors and eleven marines. Captain Dirck Haen and the merchant Isaac Gilsemans sailed on the 100-ton yacht *Zeemeuw*, with a crew of thirty-five sailors and six marines. The *de Bracq*, a small shallow-draft vessel, with Captain Jasper Jansz Koos and fourteen men, completed the expedition fleet.

Almost forty years earlier, the Dutch had heard indirectly from the Spanish on Ternate that Torres had sailed along the south coast of New Guinea on his voyage from Vanuatu to Manila. Tasman was instructed to follow the New Guinea coast to the shallow bight charted both by Willem Jansz in 1606 and Jan Carstensz in 1623 and to send the *de Bracq* into this bay to determine whether there was a passage between New Guinea and the Southland. Their instructions read:

> Cautiously cross the shallow bay situated there before sending off the galiot *de Bracq* into the bay for the space of two or three days, with the object of finding out within this vast bay any eventual passage to the South Sea.
>
> It is to be feared you will meet, in these parts, with the south-east trade winds; from which it will be difficult to keep the coast on board, if stretching to the south-east; but, notwithstanding this, endeavour by all means to proceed; so that we may be sure whether this land is divided from the Great Known South Continent, or not.

When the westerly monsoon prevails between New Guinea and Australia in December, January and February, it is technically possible to sail eastward through the Torres Strait; however, monsoonal storms could make for a difficult voyage. This was the most important part of Tasman's voyage, and if he had been able to find an eastward passage through the Torres Strait, it would have changed the history of Australia. The expedition left Banda on February 29, so if Tasman did reach the entrance to Endeavour Strait and the Rivier van Speult (Jardine River), as mapped by Jan Carstenz, it was probably too late in the season to catch the westerly winds and explore the Torres Strait. Since Tasman's Journal of this voyage has been lost, we can only speculate that the prevailing easterly winds made him conclude that a voyage from west to east through the Strait would be impossible.

The fleet now proceeded down the west coast of the Cape York Peninsula past Cape Keerweer and then to the Staten River, the furthest southerly point reached by the Carstensz expedition in 1623. From here, the VOC thought a passage south might lead to Van Diemen's Land. Tasman followed the coast of the Gulf of Carpentaria as it turned west, naming various islands and inlets, but without finding any passage to the south. Tasman's orders were to fill in the gaps between the coastlines separately discovered and named between 1606 and 1636 and look for any passages to the south or east. However, as he continued his voyage, he found a continuous northern coastline extending from the Gulf of Carpentaria all the way to the Northwest Cape in Western Australia. As a result, the Dutch discoveries of Carpentaria, Arnhems Landt, Baii van Dieman, De Wit Landt, Eendracht Landt, De Edels Landt, Landt van de Leuwin and Nuyts Landt were all joined together into the half of one continent which the Dutch declared as Hollandia Nova. However, the existence of Torres Strait was still an open question. In a letter to the VOC Directors of 23 December 1644, Van Diemen assessed the results of the voyage as follows:

> The pinnaces ... set sail from Banda on 29 February and followed the coast without finding passage between the partly explored Nova Guinea and Eendrachtsland. They sailed as far as latitude 22 2/3 degrees and longitude 119 degrees but found no through channel between the half-known Nova Guinea and the known land of the Eendracht but only found a great spacious gulf or bay as the chart and journals show. They did not discover anything important, but only found wretched naked beachcombers without rice or other valuable produce and in

many places wicked men, as your Honours will be able to learn more fully and in detail in the Batavia report ... Meanwhile this great and until now unknown Southland has been circumnavigated by the aforesaid Tasman on two voyages and the land is estimated to be 2000 miljen on the charts which we send along to Your Honours to show.

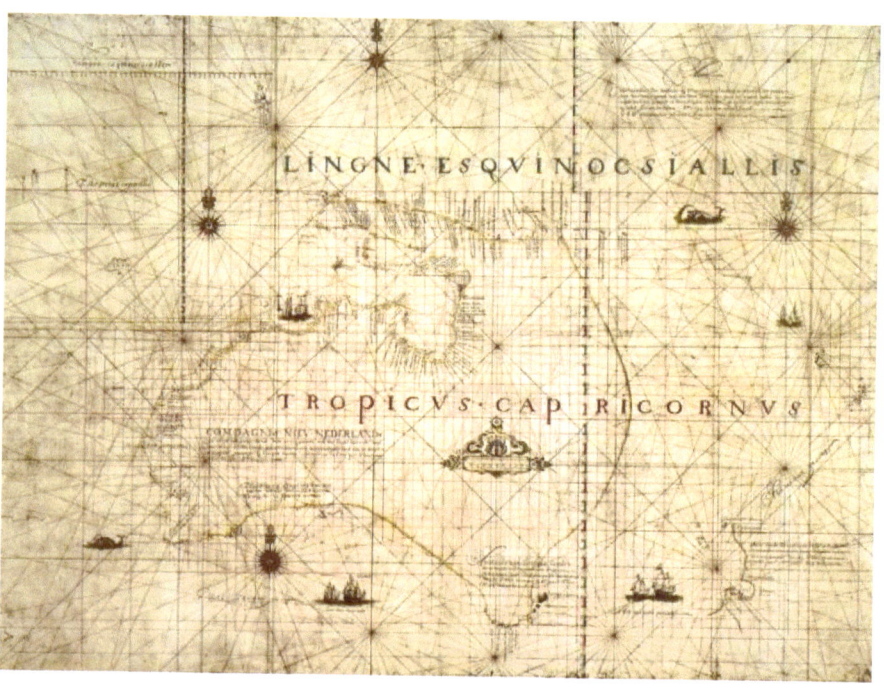

The Bonaparte Tasman Map, 1644 (enhanced version)
The State Library of NSW

There are no surviving logs or reports of this second Tasman voyage, but a display map was prepared in Batavia for the Directors of the Dutch East India Company in Amsterdam, showing the results of both of Tasman's voyages. An ornate manuscript map, drawn on delicate Japanese paper, bears just below the Tropic of Capricorn, the arms of the City of Amsterdam, showing the three crosses of St Andrew below the date 1644. The inscription in the top right-hand corner, above the line of the Equator (Lingne Esquinocsiallis) translates as:

These lands were discovered by the Company's explorers except for the northern part of New Guinea and the west of Java. This work thus put together from different writings as well as from personal observation by Abel Jansen Tasman, AD 1644, by order of His Excellency the Governor-General Antonio Van Diemen.

It was unfortunate for the Dutch that most of their discoveries were of the more barren parts of the Australian coastline, and the Company Directors in the Netherlands were not at all pleased to learn of further plans for exploration. Lacking the vision of their Governor-General in Batavia, they had, over the past few years, become increasingly alarmed by his planned voyages of discovery. Even though the Company Directors greatly respected Van Diemen for the excellent financial results he had obtained, his plans regarding future voyages of discovery and exploration caused them to lose patience. In September 1645, they wrote to Anthony van Diemen instructing him to desist from any further exploration:

We see that Your Excellency has again taken up the exploration of the coasts of Nova Guinea [the South Land] in the hope of discovering gold and silver mines there. We do not expect great things from the continuation of such explorations, which are more and more burden on the Company's resources, since they require an increase in ships and sailors. Enough lands have already been discovered for the Company to carry on its trade, provided the latter is attended by success. We do not consider it part of our task to seek out gold and silver mines for the Company, and having found such to try to derive profit from the same; such things involve a good deal more, demanding excessive expenditure and a large number of hands ... These plans of Your Excellency aim somewhat beyond our mark. The gold and silver mines that will best serve the Company's prospects, have already been found, which we deem to be our trade over the whole of the Indies.

Fortunately, van Diemen did not have to suffer the humiliation of reading these instructions. He died in Batavia in April 1645 before receiving this letter, and it can be said that the idea of further Dutch exploration of New Holland had died with him. The Australian Continent and its First Peoples then waited 125 years before another foreign ship appeared over the horizon.

5

James Cook finds a passage through the Torres Strait, 1770

This passage, which I have named Endeavour Straits, after the name of the ship, is in length north-east and south-west 10 leagues, and about 5 leagues broad, except at the north-east entrance, where it is only 2 miles broad by reason of several small Islands which lay there, one of which, called Possession Island, is of a moderate height and circuit ... laying in the middle of the south-west entrance, which we left to the southward; the depth of water we found in the Straits was from 4 to 9 fathoms.

Lieutenant James Cook, 1770

The astronomer Edmund Halley predicted that the transit of the planet Venus when it crossed between the Earth and the Sun, would occur in 1769. He argued convincingly that many careful observations of the transit, taken from widely separated points on the globe, would allow scientists to calculate the earth's distance from the sun and provide a greater understanding of the extent of the solar system. The letter from the Royal Society seeking the King's support for the expedition reads:

> To the King's Most Excellent Majesty. The Memorial of the President, Council and Fellows of the Royal Society of London for improving Natural Knowledge humbly showeth –
>
> That the passage of the Planet Venus over the Disc of the Sun, which will happen on the 3rd of June in the year 1769, is a Phaenomenon that must, if the same be accurately observed in proper places, contribute greatly to the improvement of Astronomy on which Navigation so much depends ... That the like appearance after the 3rd of June 1769 will not happen for more than 100 years ... That a correct Set of observations made in the Southern latitudes would be of greater importance than many of those made in the Northern.

James Cook's remarkable qualities as a seaman, navigator and cartographer were proven in his survey of the coast of Newfoundland, where he had carefully observed and recorded an eclipse of the sun, which allowed an accurate determination of the longitude of Newfoundland. Cook recommended that *The Earl of Pembroke*, a sturdy coal carrier, be commissioned for the voyage and renamed HMB *Endeavour*. As a merchant seaman, James Cook had learnt his trade on these tough colliers, which were stoutly built with a large storage capacity, had a flat bottom that drew comparatively little water, and could be easily careened for repair on a foreign shore when necessary.

On August 26th 1768, His Majesty's Barque *Endeavour* sailed from Plymouth harbour and, after six months, reached Tahiti and set anchor within Matavia Bay. Anchored in a calm lagoon, volcanic peaks rose above the black palm-lined beaches, and the lush green tropical vegetation of the island descended all the way down to its shores. Around them, the blue waters of its tropical lagoon were alive with native craft full of curious Tahitians. The *Endeavour* was only the third foreign ship to reach its shores, but the charms of its womenfolk were already legendary. The *Endeavour* was here to observe the Transit of Venus, but it seems that Venus, The Goddess of Love, had already reached these islands.

The British were also interested in the discovery of the mythical Terra Australis, and after their period in Tahiti and the observation of the Transit of Venus, James Cook followed his instructions from the Admiralty, and the *Endeavour* sailed south towards latitude 40 degrees in search of new land. After sailing into continuous gales, mountainous seas and the increasing cold for 2000 kilometres without sighting any land, the *Endeavour* eagerly turned west. Finally, in October 1769, they sighted land, and expectations rose. Could this be a northern promontory of the postulated Terra Australis they had been sent to discover? The crew of the *Endeavour* seemed to think it was as Joseph Banks wrote:

> At sunset all hands at the mast head, land still distant 7 or 8 leagues, appears larger than ever, in many parts 3, 4 and 5 ranges of hills are seen over the other and a chain of Mountains over all, some of which appear enormously high. Much difference of opinion and many conjectures about islands, rivers etc, but all hands seem to agree that this is certainly the Continent we are in search of.

After the *Endeavour* circumnavigated the North and South Islands, it proved to be Staten Landt (New Zealand) that Abel Tasman had encountered in 1642. Banks describes how Cook proved 'the total demolition of our aerial fabric called a continent' and how the southern continent now seems more myth than reality. This meant the abandonment of their search for Terra Australis and Banks wrote:

> This for my own part I confess I could not do without much regret – That a Southern Continent really exists, I firmly believe; but if asked why I believe so, I confess my reasons are

weak; yet I have a prepossession in favour of the fact which I find it difficult to account for.

Having now completed his instructions from the Admiralty, Lieutenant Cook had to decide how they would return to England. Forever the explorer, he wanted to search for the undiscovered east coast of New Holland, unknown anywhere north of Van Diemen's Land as named by Abel Tasman. Cook wrote in his journal:

> Being now resolved to quit this Country altogether and to bend my thoughts towards returning home by such a route as might Conduce to the advantage of the Service I am upon, I consulted with the Officers upon the most Eligible way of putting them in Execution. To return by way of Cape Horn was what I most wished, because by this route we should have been able to prove the existence or non-existence of a Southern Continent which yet remains doubtful; but in order to ascertain this we must have kept in a higher Latitude in the very Depth of Winter but the Condition of the Ship, in every respect was not thought sufficient for such an Undertaking. For the same reason, thoughts of proceeding directly to the Cape of Good Hope were laid aside, especially as no Discovery of any moment could be hoped for in that route. It was therefore decided to return by way of the Indies by the following route: upon leaving this coast to steer westwards until we fall in with the East Coast of New Holland and then follow the direction of that coast to the northward or what other direction it may take until we arrive at its northern extremity.

In April 1770, after three months sailing west, Cook first sighted the unknown east coast of Australia near the eastern extremity of Victoria at what he named Cape Hicks after the crewman who first sighted land:

> With the first day light, this morn the Land was seen, at 10 it

was pretty plainly observed; it is made in sloping hills, covered in part with trees or bushed but interspersed with large tracts of sand.

In the afternoon, the crew saw smoke in several places, which led them to believe the country was inhabited. Sailing northward for almost ten days, the *Endeavour* could not find a harbour or safe place to land on the surf-washed coast. Finally, they rounded a Cape and found a sheltered anchorage in a large bay:

> The land this morn appeared cliffy and barren without wood. An opening appearing like a harbour was seen and we stood directly in for it. A small smoke arising from a very barren place we directed our glasses that way and we soon saw about 10 people, who on our approach left the fire and retired to a little prominence where they could conveniently see the ship.

The *Endeavour* remained in the bay for a week. The Union Jack was flown every day, and an inscription was cut into one of the trees with the name of the *Endeavour* and the date of its arrival. The botanists Joseph Banks and Daniel Solander collected the leaves of many plants previously unknown to science. Plants that had evolved on this vast continent over its 30 million years of isolation after it broke off from Gondwana Land. Initially, Cook had thought to name it Stingray Bay because of the abundance of them in its shallow waters, however, on their last day, he wrote:

> Sunday 6th. In the evening the yawl returned from fishing having caught two Sting rays weighing near 600 pounds. The great quantity of new plants which Mr Banks and Dr Solander collected in this place occasioned me giving it the name of Botany Bay.

After a week at Botany Bay, the *Endeavour* sailed out between what is now known as Cape Banks and Cape Solander and turned north along the coast. As they continued their voyage northwards, the *Endeavour* and its crew were sailing into a trap. The Great Barrier Reef stretches over 2300 kilometres from near Hervey Bay to the northernmost point of Australia and almost to the coast of New Guinea. The gap between the coast and the reef was widest in the south and gradually narrowed as they sailed north. On the 9th of June, Cook had taken the risk of sailing at night, under a full moon, when at 11 pm the *Endeavour* ran aground and as Cook explains:

> Having the advantage of fine breeze of wind and a clear moon-light night ... we deepened our water from 14 to 21 fathom when all at once we fell into 12, 10 and 8 fathom. At this time I had everybody at their stations to put about and come to an anchor but in this I was not so fortunate for meeting again with deep water I thought there could be no danger in standing on, before 10 o'clock we had 20 and 21 fathom and continued in that depth until a few minutes before 11 and before the man at the lead could heave another cast, the Ship struck and stuck fast.

The *Endeavour* had run aground on a coral reef, which had punched a hole in the vessel, and she was rapidly taking on water. Cannon, ballast, lead and coal were tossed overboard in a futile attempt to float the ship off the coral. Cook later estimated that the crew cast overboard 40-50 tons of weight. All the crew, including Banks and his party, worked the pumps all that night, all the next day and again the following night while trying to keep their vessel afloat. Banks describes their ordeal:

> At night the tide almost floated her but she made waters so fast that three pumps hard worked could but just keep her clear and the 4th absolutely refused to deliver a drop of water. Now in my opinion I entirely gave up the ship and packing up what I thought I might save prepared myself for the worst ... if (as

was probable) she should make more water when hauled off she must sink and we well knew that our boats were not capable of carrying us all ashore, so that some, probably the most of us must be drowned. Fear of death now stared us in the face; hopes we had none but of being able to keep the ship afloat till we could run her ashore.

Joseph Banks, 11 June 1770

To their great relief, the *Endeavour* floated off on the next high tide, and the pumps could still hold the leak. Cook sent the pinnace ahead to try and find a suitable landing place where they could inspect and repair the damage or, if necessary, build a vessel that would carry some of the crew to Timor for help. Banks describes the discovery of Endeavour River as providential for the winds had started to blow, and the ship may have sunk had she stayed out a day longer:

> The Captain and myself went ashore to view the Harbour and found it indeed beyond our most sanguine wishes: it was the mouth of a river the entrance of which was to be sure narrow enough and shallow, but once in the ship might be moored afloat so near the shore ... that all her Cargo might be got out and in again in a very short time.

Repairing the Endeavour at Endeavour River,
Sydney Parkinson, University of Pittsburgh Library

After careening the *Endeavour*, an inspection of her hull found a hole large enough to have sunk the ship, but fortune had worked in their favour as the hole had been plugged with a piece of coral as big as a man's fist. Sydney Parkinson wrote:

> The same rock, therefore, that endangered us, yielded us the principle means of our redemption; for, had not this fragment not intruded into the leak, in all probability the ship would have sunk.

It would take at least a week to repair the vessel so sleeping tents, storage tents, a blacksmith forge, a carpenter's workshop and pens for the animals were set up on shore. Banks and Solander began collecting specimens. Fortunately, the 'gum' trees were now in flower, and Parkinson sketched two species of Eucalyptus, the smooth white-barked *Eucalyptus alba* and the narrow-leaved red ironbark, *Eucalyptus crebra*. These were the only examples of eucalypts collected during their time in Australia, and Parkinson describes the 'very grateful odour' coming from a fire of burning eucalypts, a smell that was so familiar to the aborigines and to the many subsequent generations of Australian settlers.

A hunting party sent to the other side of the river encountered an unusual animal described as large as a greyhound, of a mouse colour and very swift. Banks went out on a subsequent hunt and describes his encounter with this strange animal:

> With first dawn we set out in search of Game. We walked many miles over the flats and saw four of the animals, two of which my greyhound fairly chased, but they beat him owing to the length and thickness of the grass which prevented him from running while they at every bound leaped over the tops of it. We observed much to our surprise that instead of going on all fours this animal went only on two legs, making vast bounds.

Next, Banks describes how the second lieutenant was able to shoot one of the animals, which had long been the subject of their speculation. Banks wrote 'kanguru' in his diary, his anglicised version of the aboriginal word 'ganurru'. The animal weighed twenty-eight pounds and was eaten for dinner, providing what was described as excellent food, although Banks fails to mention if its bones were preserved for science.

During their stay at Endeavour River, the crew made almost daily contact with the local aborigines, but they generally kept out of each other's way. The natives here used outrigger canoes, which were an improvement on the bark canoes the aborigines had used in Botany Bay. They mainly caught fish, stingrays, and turtles, which were also the main food sources being gathered by the stranded sailors.

An important cultural protocol was not understood by the crew, as the turtle they collected should have been shared with the Aboriginal community. The aborigines had found twelve large turtles in one of the boats, some of which they attempted to haul off but were immediately resisted by Cook and the crew. The sharing code was broken, and the aborigines retaliated by taking a stick from the fire and lighting the dry grass around the campsite. Cook took a musket and shot at one of the men, drawing blood. Later, an aboriginal leader sought reconciliation and as described by Banks:

> He came forward to us carrying ... a lance without a point. He halted several times and employed himself in collecting the moisture from under his armpit with his finger which he every time drew through his mouth. We beckoned him to come: he then spoke to the others who all laid their lances against a tree and leaving them came forward.

Having completed their repairs and after 47 days ashore, the *Endeavour* and its crew were ready to continue their voyage north. They needed to find a proper shipyard to repair the *Endeavour* before she could safely return to England. The nearest shipyard was at the port of

Batavia on the island of Java in the Dutch East Indies. However, first, they had to find their way out of the shoals and reefs that surrounded them, and Banks wrote in his journal:

> Where to go? – to windward was impossible, to leeward was a labyrinth of shoals, so that how soon might we have the ship to repair again, or lose her, quite no one could tell.

For the next week, the *Endeavour* threaded its way through the labyrinth of shoals with the pinnace sounding the water depth ahead of them. Eventually, they reached Lizard Island, where Cook could climb to the highest point and observe what lay ahead:

> I immediately went upon the highest hill on the island where to my mortification I discovered a Reef of Rocks lying at about 2 or 3 Leagues without the island, extending in a line NW and SE farther than I could see and on which the sea broke very high.

Fortunately, Cook could see a gap in the line of breakers, which might allow a way out through the Barrier Reef. He sent the pinnace ahead to sound the narrow channel, which allowed the *Endeavour* to pass through into the open ocean. Banks describes the Barrier Reef as:

> Something scarcely known in Europe but is a wall of coral rock where the large waves of the vast ocean meeting with so sudden a resistance as to make a terrible mountainous surf, especially in our case where the general trade wind blows directly upon it.

To their great relief, they were now safe in deep water outside the reef, free of all fears of shoals and running aground again. The safest known route to Batavia would be the route that William Dampier in the *Roebuck* had charted in 1699 through the Dampier Passage between the island he named New Britain and New Guinea and then along the north coast of Papua New Guinea. However, fate was to decide otherwise. Cook did not want to sail too far out to sea in case he missed sighting the supposed passage between New Holland and New Guinea as discovered by Torres. However, three days later, a strong easterly current was driving them back towards the Barrier Reef and the line of breakers from which they had just escaped.

The French explorer Louis Antoine de Bougainville, with his frigate *La Boudeuse*, approached the Barrier Reef directly from the east in June 1776. The tremendous roar of the surf breaking across the reef gave Bougainville enough warning to haul away. Describing the roar of the surf and their lucky escape, he wrote, 'This was the voice of God, and we obeyed'.

At daybreak, the roar of the surf was plainly heard by James Cook, and the foaming breakers could be seen only a few miles away. There was no wind to allow them to haul away, and the ocean current relentlessly carried the *Endeavour* towards the outer edge of the Barrier Reef. Joseph Banks describes their situation as desperate:

> At three o'clock this morn it dropped calm on a sudden which did not at all better our situation; we judged ourselves not more than 4 or 5 leagues from the reef, maybe much less, and the swell of the sea which drove right in upon it carried the ship towards it fast ... as day broke the vast foaming billows were plainly enough to be seen scarce a mile from us and towards which we found the ship carried by the waves surprisingly fast ... Now was our case truly desperate, no man I believe but who gave himself entirely over, a speedy death was all we had to hope for and that from the vastness of the breakers which must quickly dash the ship all to pieces - was scarce to be doubted.

They were now almost upon the reef. Cook describes how the ship rose up to a prodigious height with one breaker, and that between them and destruction was only a dismal valley the breadth of one wave.

Then, what Banks describes as a little breeze came up from the west, which allowed them to use their sails to move in a slanting direction away from the Barrier Reef until they saw a narrow break in the reef ahead. The pinnace was sent to scout the opening and came back with the news that although it was very narrow, the passage was quite free from shoals. Banks describes how they were again saved from certain disaster:

> The ship's head was immediately put towards it and with the tide she ran fast so that by three we entered and were hurried in by a stream almost like a mill race, which kept us from even a fear of the sides, though it was not above ¼ of a mile in breadth. By 4pm we came to an anchor happy once more to encounter those shoals which but two days before we thought ourselves supremely happy to have escaped from. How little do men know what is for their real advantage: two days ago our utmost wishes were crowned by getting without the reef and today we were made happy again by getting within it.

For once, James Cook allowed his emotions to be recorded in his journal because he wrote that it pleased GOD at this juncture to send a light air of wind, and he named the gap in the reef Providential Channel.

In 1769 the British geographer Alexander Dalrymple, whilst translating some Spanish documents obtained after the British capture of Manila, found a copy of Luís Vaz de Torres' long-forgotten letter to the King of Spain, detailing his voyage along the south coast of New Guinea. A map of Pacific voyages, which indicated the voyage thought to be made between New Holland and Papua-New Guinea by Torres, had been included in Dalrymple's 'An account of the discoveries made in the South Pacific previous to 1764'.

Now inside the Great Barrier Reef, Cook's voyage west would require a voyage through the uncharted Torres Strait. Cook would have had few details of Torres's voyage through the Strait except a general map provided by the Admiralty hydrographer Alexander Dalrymple. Would James Cook have known that Torres had spent thirty-four days amidst reefs and shoals before his vessels finally found a way through the Torres Strait? Would James Cook have known the Torres had to invent a new method of sailing before he could finally find a way through the reefs and shoals of the Strait?

On August 21, the *Endeavour* reached the northern extent of the Australian mainland. With the pinnace scouting the way ahead, the *Endeavour* passed through the Adolphus Channel and towards the northern point of the mainland. Cook wrote:

> The point of the Main, which forms one side of the Passage before mentioned, and which is the Northern Promontory of this Country, I have named York Cape, in honour of his late Royal Highness, the Duke of York.

After rounding Cape York, James Cook could see open water south of what he named Prince of Wales Island; thinking he had found a passage through the strait, he decided to land on what he later named Possession Island. On 22 August, he wrote:

> Gentle breezes at East by South and clear weather. We had not steered above 3 or 4 Miles along shore to the westward before we discovered the land ahead to be Islands detached by several Channels from the mainland; upon this we brought to wait for the Yawl, and called the other Boats on board, and after giving them proper instructions, sent them away again to lead us through the channel next to the Main ... Between these 2 points we could see no land, so that we were in great hopes that we had at last found out a passage into the Indian Seas; but in order to be better informed I landed with a party of men, accompanied by Mr. Banks and Dr. Solander, upon the Island which lies at the South-East point of the Passage.

This was Tuined (Possession Island), one of the inner islands of the Torres Strait and closest to the mainland. Cook led a party of Banks, Solander and one marine to the island's summit, from where he was delighted to confirm there was open water ahead and to know that he had found his way through the Torres Strait. The crew waited on the ship for a signal that the way was clear. Eventually, Cook held aloft the signal flag and ordered the marine to fire three signal shots:

> Having satisfied myself of the great probability of a passage, through which I intend going with the ship, and therefore may land no more upon this Eastern coast of New Holland, and on the Western side I can make no new discovery, the honour of which belongs to the Dutch Navigators, but the Eastern Coast from the Latitude of 38 degrees South to this place, I am confident, was never seen or visited by any European before us; and notwithstanding I had in the name of his Majesty taken possession of several places upon this Coast, I now once more hoisted English Colours, and in the Name of His Majesty King George the Third took possession of the whole Eastern coast from the above Latitude to this place by the name of New Wales, together with all the Bays, Harbours, Rivers, and Islands, situated upon the said Coast; after which we fired 3 volleys of small arms, which were answered by the like number from the ship.

Cook had made another discovery at Cape York because he saw several people armed with a bow and arrows instead of the spears he had seen previously on the Australian mainland. Furthermore, he had seen two or three men wearing large breastplates, which he supposed were made of pearl oyster shells. These were features new to Cook, it suggested a different race of people, and it is significant that a polished pearl shell, suspended around the neck, is still worn by the Torres Strait Islanders for their traditional ceremonies and dances. Cook wrote:

> We saw upon all the Adjacent Lands and Islands a great

number of smokes - a certain sign that they are inhabited - and we have daily seen smokes on every part of the coast we have lately been upon. Between 7 and 8 o'clock a.m. we saw several naked people, all or most of them women, down upon the beach picking up shells, etc.; they had not a single rag of any kind of clothing upon them, and both these and those we saw yesterday were in every respect the same sort of people we have seen everywhere upon the coast. However, 2 or 3 of the men we saw yesterday had on large breastplates, which we supposed were made of pearl oyster shells; this was a thing, as well as the bow and arrows, we had not seen before.

Modern DNA studies show that the Australian Aborigines are our planet's oldest continuously living population. They migrated from Africa around 75,000 years ago and would have reached Australia by island hopping across the Indonesian archipelago during the lowering of sea levels and they have been living in Australia for at least 65,000 years. Before the departure of the *Endeavour* from England, Lord Morton, as the President of the Royal Society, provided Cook and Banks with a set of suggestions on how they should conduct themselves during their encounters with local inhabitants and strongly argued for the land rights of the Indigenous people to be upheld:

> They are the natural and in the strictest sense of the word, the legal possessors of the several regions they inhabit. No European Nation has a right to occupy any part of their country or settle among them without their voluntary consent. Conquest over such people can give no just title because they could never be the Aggressors. They may naturally and justly attempt to repel intruders, whom they may apprehend are come to disturb them in their quiet possession of their country, whether that apprehension be well or ill founded.
>
> Lord Morton, 10 August 1768

James Cook admired the Aborigines he encountered and their lifestyle, and before departing Australia, he wrote:

> From what I have said of the natives of New Holland they may appear to some to be the most wretched people upon Earth, but in reality, they are far happier than we Europeans; Being wholly unacquainted not only with the superfluous but the necessary conveniences so sought after in Europe, they are happy in not knowing the use of them ... In short they seemed to set no value upon anything we gave them, nor would they part with anything of their own for any one article we could offer them; this in my opinion argues that they think themselves provided with all the necessaries of life and that they have no superfluities.

Cook had now achieved his objective of exploring the previously undiscovered east coast of New Holland and by navigating a passage between New Holland and New Guinea, and he wrote:

> This passage, which I have named Endeavour Straits, after the name of the ship, is in length north-east and south-west 10 leagues, and about 5 leagues broad, except at the north-east entrance, where it is only 2 miles broad by reason of several small Islands which lay there, one of which, called Possession Island, is of a moderate height and circuit ... laying in the middle of the south-west entrance, which we left to the southward; the depth of water we found in the Straits was from 4 to 9 fathoms.

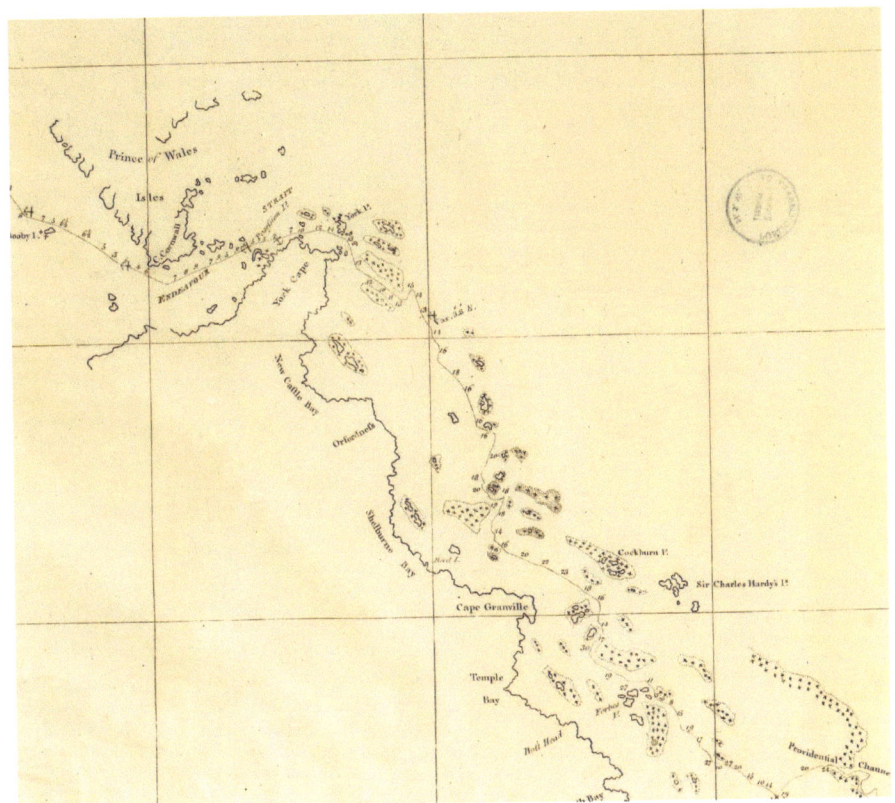

Chart of the sea coast of New South Wales or the east coast of New Holland, 1775 (detail)
James Cook, British Library, London

Cook wrote that he hoped a less hazardous passage through the Torres Strait would be discovered. In fact, he had found the simplest passage from the Inner Reef around Cape York out into the Arafura Sea through what he named Endeavour Strait and had made this passage in only three days. The Endeavour's last stop was at a barren rock frequented by birds, and after briefly going ashore, Cook named it Booby Island. After so many years at sea and after almost twice being shipwrecked on the Barrier Reef, they were now, to the relief of all on board in charted waters and sailing for home. Banks felt the same relief as all the crew, and as they left the Endeavour Strait, he wrote:

As soon as the boat was hoisted in, we made sail and steered away from this land to the no small satisfaction of I believe three fourths of our company, the sick became well and the melancholy looked gay. The greatest part of them were now pretty far gone with the longing for home which the physicians have gone so far as to esteem a disease under the name of nostalgia; indeed I can find hardly anybody in the ship clear of its effects but the Captain, Dr Solander and myself, indeed we three have pretty constant employment for our minds which I believe to be the best if not the only remedy for it.

The engraved charts of the *Endeavour* voyage by James Cook (surveyor) and Isaac Smith (chart maker) were published in 1773, along with John Hawkesworth's documentation of the voyage, entitled *An Account of the Voyages Undertaken by the Orders of His Present Majesty, for Making Discoveries in the Southern Hemisphere.* The chart shown here has the voyage of the Endeavour from the Providential Channel to the Endeavour Strait.

6

Timor and Kupang (Coepang)

The location of the Dutch settlement of Kupang on the western end of the island of Timor was crucial for European sailors shipwrecked in the region of the Torres Strait. It was the nearest European settlement and a port of refuge that could be reached in two weeks' sailing in the ship's boats. However, the *Endeavour* needed extensive repairs, and James Cook knew that this could only be done in the capital of the Dutch East India Company at Batavia (Jakarta).

Around 1649, the Dominican friar Antonio de Sao Jacinto sailed across from Flores to establish a Catholic mission in West Timor, where he decided to settle in Kupang because of its natural harbour and strategic position. Having some success at converting the islanders to Christianity, he began the construction of a small church and fort, which he located on a promontory and adjacent to a stream running into the bay. This had not progressed very far before it was captured by the Dutch East India Company in 1653 without a shot being fired. Since the Dutch now intended to take control of Timor and the sandalwood trade from the Portuguese, they completed the construction of the fort, which they named Fort Concordia.

At the furthest end of the Dutch seaborne empire, the men obliged to serve in the Dutch garrison had probably been banished from elsewhere, and a visiting Company official described them as:

> Leading from the highest to the lowest, a vile and irregular life, both in drunkenness and in whoring, wherein their commander, Culenberg, sets them an example like a true captain.

Although it has an excellent harbour, Kupang lies at the edge of an infertile plain, and the sandalwood trees that the Dutch East India Company sought to control grew far away in the mountains of the interior. Mountains that were controlled by the Portuguese traders from Larantuka in Flores. The Dutch decided to set this right, and a strong military force arrived in 1656 to assert Dutch control over West Timor. Led by the celebrated General Arnold de Vlamingh, he and his forces marched from Kupang into the hinterland, where in the mountains of Amarassi they encountered a determined and well-armed enemy with a strategic plan of attack. The Dutch forward party lost eight dead and forty-six wounded in the ambush. Their troops turned to retreat but were confined to a narrow mountain path, and their route is described as follows:

> We had to walk in single file if we wished to escape uninjured; this put us at a disadvantage, which the enemy turned to his own advantage, and after sending down a shower of spears on us assaulted us like lightning, stabbing some of us in the back ... Nay, what is more they carried off by force Gerritt Gerritsen from the midst of his company, with banner and all, and seized the drummer's drum, and there was nothing we could do to stop them.

Forced to withdraw in confusion to the shelter of Fort Concordia, General de Vlamingh lost 170 Dutch soldiers and even more of his native troops in this encounter, and his reputation was shattered. The Directors of the Dutch East India Company realised their access to the sandalwood trade had been lost to the Portuguese and decided to abandon Fort Concordia, stating:

> And as from now on there will be little in the way of trade for us in the area of Timor, and the sandal trade has been lost, so that there will be more expenses to incur than profits to gain for the Honourable Company, it has been resolved, in accordance with the written instructions of the distinguished Lords Seventeen, to abandon the fortresses Henricus and Concordia, these being sufficiently unprofitable.

However, Fort Concordia continued in Dutch hands, and for the next one hundred years, the Dutch East India Company secured their position in West Timor by forming alliances with Timorese leaders of the small states around the Bay of Kupang and on the islands of Roti and Savu. We have a description of Kupang in 1669 by the English explorer William Dampier, where he found a neat little church and, within the walls of the fort, a garrison of about 50 Dutch soldiers with a similar number of native troops, along with a well-supplied vegetable garden.

In 1749, the Portuguese traders decided to drive the Dutch intruders off West Timor and gathered their forces to attack Fort Concordia. The Dutch commander of the Fort was surprised by the sudden appearance of one of his tributary Timorese chiefs giving warning of a multitude of armed men marching towards Kupang. The Portuguese traders and their Timorese allies, led by Lieutenant-General Gaspar da Costa, Provincial Lieutenant Pasqual da Costa and Provincial Sergeant Major Amaro da Costa, were marching towards Kupang to the beat of their military drummers and bearing the King of Portugal's flag, standard and banner.

The Hollanders hurriedly put together a force consisting of 23 Dutch soldiers, 130 Dutch-trained Ambonese troops, 240 Savunese and 30

Rotinese troops and a large number of their Timorese tribal allies. This unlikely force marched out of Fort Concordia to attack the Portuguese traders who, having lost the element of surprise, were now ensconced in a stone-walled encampment on the plain of Penfui outside Kupang. The battle raged all day and proved to be a turning point in Timorese history when the Dutch East Indies Company, with their local allies, drove back the Portuguese and their allies, inflicting heavy casualties. Gaspar da Costa was killed in the battle, and according to a Dutch report, he was:

> Struck down by a Timorese with a spear and immediately beheaded like those killed before him. Although it is difficult to estimate their number it is at any rate certain that, that very evening the Timorese carried off in triumph approximately a thousand heads and at least as many again in the course of the next two days, while they are still relentlessly pursuing the enemy.

From this time, the Dutch began to extend their control over the western part of Timor towards the current boundaries with East Timor. Even with the defeat of the Portuguese on the plains of Penfui and their new alliances with the Timorese in the western part of the island, the Dutch could never make inroads into the sandalwood trade from their distant base in Kupang.

Although the Dutch claimed to have control over the west and south sides of Timor, their influence was limited to the town, which consisted of little more than two parallel dirt streets stretching along the southern side of Kupang Bay and lined with Chinese-owned houses, shops and warehouses. The dwellings of the handful of Dutch administrators were clustered around a square behind the town where the Resident had a large government house, and there was also a Dutch church and a school.

In due course, Kupang became a popular victualling port for whalers who used it as their home base while hunting whales in the Savu and Timor Seas. Fresh water could be obtained from a pipe on the beach, and fowl, coconuts, and bananas were on sale at the local markets. Rum was available from the Chinese trade stores for the sailors, but it was expensive. The locally fermented palm liquor was a better option, as it was cheap and suitably potent.

View of the harbour, the town and the Dutch fort at Coepang, 1807
Charles Alexandre Leseur

On June 14, 1789, a British vessel arrived in Kupang harbour. Its commander went ashore to determine whether the Dutch would welcome a British naval vessel. Leaving his men on watch, he staggered up the beach to the small stone fort built on a rocky promontory. In Fort Concordia, the Dutch Governor was shocked by the spectre of death that stood before him, its hair and beard long and matted, its eyes sunk back into its skull, and its flesh wasted away until only skin and bone remained. This was Lieutenant William Bligh, who, together with 18 of his men, had been cast adrift in the middle of the Pacific Ocean after the mutiny on his ship *Bounty*. With only a pittance of food and supplies, Bligh and his men had sailed their 23-foot open boat 6000 kilometres across the Pacific Ocean and through the Torres Strait to reach this nearest outpost of European civilisation in only six weeks.

It takes six weeks for a healthy person to die of starvation, but sustained by limited ship food as well as shellfish and some seabirds, William Bligh and his loyal seamen had made one of the greatest open boat voyages in maritime history.

7

Mutiny - William Bligh and the Bounty, 1789

> God damn you, you scoundrels, you are all thieves alike, and combine with the men to rob me – I suppose you'll steal my yams next, but I'll sweat you for it, you rascals, I'll make half of you jump overboard before you get through Endeavour Straits.
>
> Lieutenant William Bligh, *HMS Bounty*

During their stay in Tahiti, Cook, Banks, Solander, and the crew of the *Endeavour* regularly dined on breadfruit, which grew everywhere and was the staple food of the island. A good food source, it is rich in carbohydrates, rich in vitamin C, as well as thiamine and potassium. According to Daniel Solander:

> The Breadfruit of the South Sea Islands within the Tropics, which was by us during several months, daily eaten as a substitute for Bread, was universally esteemed as palatable and nourishing as Bread itself; no one of the whole ship company

complained when served with Breadfruit in lieu of Biscuit; and from the health and strength of whole nations whose principal food it is, I didn't scruple to call it one of the most useful vegetables in the world ... As it undoubtedly must be of the utmost consequence to bring so valuable a Fruit to countries where the climate is favourable to encourage everybody who goes to any part of the world where it is to be met with, bring it over either by young plants properly rooted or by seeds collected in the Proper season, and sown during the passage. I am sure no expense ought to be spared in an undertaking so interesting to the public.

The Breadfruit Tree, 1796
J.Wilkes

Annual sugar consumption in Britain increased from about 2 pounds per head in 1650 to 90 pounds by the early 20th century, which was about half the sugar that reached Europe. The slaves working the Caribbean sugar plantations had to be fed, and in 1787, London merchants and planters with West Indian possessions proposed that an Admiralty vessel be sent to Tahiti to collect breadfruit seedlings and transport them to the West Indies, where they could be grown to feed the plantation slaves.

The Admiralty purchased a 215-ton coastal trading vessel to be converted into a floating greenhouse and renamed it the *Bounty*. The whole lower deck was modified, and five rows of shelving were installed to house the pot plants. Beneath a false floor, the deck was lined with lead to collect the precious freshwater runoff and allow it to be recycled. Skylights were installed to provide the necessary sunlight, and gratings mounted on the deck ensured ventilation.

This was thirty-three-year-old Lieutenant William Bligh's first voyage in command. The second in command was the Master, John Fryer, with three warrant officers, one surgeon, two master's mates, two midshipmen, and thirty-four petty officers and seamen, making a crew of forty-four, to which were added two gardeners to care for the breadfruit seedlings.

The horticultural importance of this voyage meant that David Nelson, as a gardener, was appointed even before the captain himself. Nelson had served with Cook on his third expedition to the Pacific and returned to Kew Gardens with more than 200 packets of seeds. He worked at Kew for the next seven years until Joseph Banks appointed him to serve on this new expedition.

Much about the *Bounty* voyage was unusual for the Navy. The Navy saw this voyage as a civilian mission, as a cost-saving measure and because of the lack of space, there were no marines to enforce the captain's authority, as was normally the case. Bligh was also the only commissioned officer on the vessel, which meant there was no hierarchy of officers between the Captain and his Master or a complement of marines to help enforce his command. This was Bligh's first command, and he had to take full responsibility for the discipline of the crew as well as the navigation and running of the ship. This could easily be described as an accident waiting to happen, which, together with Bligh's raging temper and foul mouth, created the conditions for mutiny.

The *Bounty* left Spithead on 23 December 1787 and soon ran into a North Atlantic storm, breaking spars and halyards and washing some supplies overboard. At some time during the voyage, Bligh's temper caused a confrontation with the Master, John Fryer, resulting in Bligh bypassing him and giving these responsibilities to Fletcher Christian, who had served with him in both the Navy and the British Merchant Marine and who Bligh had nominated for this voyage. For three weeks, the *Bounty* struggled with the tempestuous seas around Cape Horn and then lost valuable time sailing east to the Cape of Good Hope before crossing the Southern Ocean to Van Diemen's Land and entering the Pacific Ocean. The *Bounty* reached Tahiti on 27 October 1788. The first problem they encountered was that the young breadfruit seedlings were not sufficiently developed to survive the voyage to the West Indies, and they had to wait for some months. Bligh should have recognised the situation and left on a voyage of exploration. However, his orders were precise, and he would have to wait in Tahiti. Joseph Banks, during his visit on the *Endeavour*, had described what he believed to be the islanders' favourite occupation:

> In the Island of Otaheite where Love is the Chief Occupation, the favourite, nay almost the Sole Luxury of the inhabitants; both the bodies and souls of the women are modelled into the utmost perfection for the soft science, idleness, the father of Love reigns here in almost unmolested ease. While we inhabitants of a changeable climate are obliged to Plow, Sow, Harrow, Reap, Thrash, Grind, Knead and Bake our daily bread and each revolving year again to Plow, Sow etc. etc. the Tahitian has but to climb the breadfruit tree and this Leisure is given up to Love.

The five months waiting in Tahiti would prove disastrous for William Bligh as Fletcher Christian and the crew of the *Bounty* formed relationships with the Tahitian women, and naval discipline virtually disappeared. The breadfruit seedlings were eventually ready to be loaded, and over one thousand plants were carried to the *Bounty*. Bligh's self-denial in the face of the island's temptations may have influenced his anger and disapproval of Fletcher Christian, who he had recently promoted to acting Lieutenant. Before their departure, Bligh wrote:

> Today, all the plants were on board, being in seven hundred and seventy-four pots, thirty-nine tubs, and twenty-four boxes. The number of bread-fruit plants were one thousand and fifteen; besides which, we had collected a number of other plants.

The *Bounty* sailed from Tahiti on 5 April 1789 and headed west into the Pacific. According to their instructions from the Admiralty, they were to voyage through the Torres Strait to the Cape of Good Hope to keep the precious breadfruit seedlings in a tropical climate for as long as possible. Bligh knew this would be a dangerous passage as he would have to find a way across the Barrier Reef and then find his way through the islands and reefs of the Torres Strait. For this reason, he had a copy of the maps and the log of Captain Cook's voyage from almost twenty years earlier.

The boatswain's mate, James Morrison, wrote that Bligh failed to appear on deck until noon on a certain morning, suggesting that some physical affliction severely incapacitated him. When he did appear, he was in a raging temper. Taking a turn around the quarterdeck, he discovered that some coconuts he had bought were missing and believed they could not have been taken without the officers noticing. All of them denied knowledge of the theft, and as Morrison reports, Bligh proclaimed, "Then you must have taken them yourselves" and questioned them individually. Fletcher Christian answered the query with, "I do not know, Sir, but I hope you don't think me so mean as to be guilty of stealing yours". Bligh responded:

> "Yes, you damned hound I do – you must have stolen them from me or you could have given a better account of them – God damn you, you scoundrels, you are all thieves alike and combine with the men to rob me – I suppose you'll steal my yams next, but I'll sweat you for it, you rascals, I'll make half of you jump overboard before you get through Endeavour Straits".

Bligh had branded Christian as a thief and a liar in front of the entire ship's company, which would have consequences. The *Bounty* had sailed almost 2000 kilometres to the west and reached the vicinity of Tofoa, one of the small islands of Tonga. According to Bligh, all appeared well, and he later wrote:

> The morning of the 28th April, the north-westernmost of the Friendly Islands, called Tofoa, bearing north-east, I was steering to the westward with a ship in most perfect order, all my plants in a most flourishing condition, all my men and officers in good health, and in short, everything to flatter and insure my most sanguine expectations. On leaving the deck I gave directions for the course to be steered during the night. John Fryer had the first watch; the gunner the middle watch; and Fletcher Christian the morning watch. This was the turn of duty for the night.

Fletcher Christian led the mutiny, and just before sunrise the following day, he, together with Charles Churchill, the masters' mate, John Mills, the gunners' mate, and Thomas Burkitt, a seaman, entered Bligh's cabin. Armed with muskets and bayonets, they seized him, tied his hands behind his back and brought him on deck. The mutiny on the *Bounty* had begun and Bligh later wrote:

> I demanded the reason of such violence, but received no other answer than abuse, for not holding my tongue. The master, the gunner, Mr. Elphinstone, the master's mate, and Nelson, were kept confined below; and the fore-hatchway was guarded by sentinels. The boatswain and carpenter, and also Mr. Samuel the clerk, were allowed to come upon deck, where they saw me standing abaft the mizen-mast, with my hands tied behind my back, under a guard, with Christian at their head. The boatswain was ordered to hoist the launch out, with a threat that if he did not do it instantly, he would have to take care of himself.

Those loyal seamen who were to go in the launch with Bligh were allowed to collect twine, canvas, lines, sails, cordage, eight casks of water, one hundred and fifty pounds of bread, and a small quantity of rum and wine. Also, a quadrant and compass were allowed, but maps and a timekeeper were forbidden. Bligh writes how his clerk tried to save some of his most precious items:

> To Mr. Samuel, the clerk, I am indebted for securing my journals and commission, with some material ship papers. Without these I had nothing to certify what I had done, and my honour and character might have been suspected, without my possessing a proper document to have defended them. All this he did with great resolution, though guarded and strictly watched. He attempted to save the timekeeper, and a box with my surveys, drawings, and remarks, for fifteen years past, which were numerous; when he was hurried away with "Damn your eyes, you are well off to get what you have".

Captain Bligh leaving the Bounty after the Mutiny
C.J.Staniland

Eighteen men, loyal to Bligh or to the Royal Navy and not wishing to be branded as mutineers, joined Bligh in the twenty-three-foot launch. They were John Fryer the Master; Thomas Ledward the surgeon; David Nelson the botanist, William Peckover the gunner, William Cole the boatswain, William Purcell the carpenter, William Elphistone the Master's Mate, Thomas Hayward a midshipman, John Hallet a midshipman, John Norton the quartermaster, Peter Lenkletter a quartermaster, George Simpson the quartermaster's mate, Lawrence Lebogue the sailmaker, the cooks John Smith and Thomas Hall, Robert Lamb the butcher, John Samuel the clerk and Robert Tinkler a ship's boy. The launch was already overloaded, and Joseph Coleman an armourer; Michael Byrne an able seaman, the carpenter's mates Thomas McIntosh and Charles Norman, were ordered by Bligh to remain on the ship for lack of space in the open boat. He called out to those still loyal - "You can't all go with me, lads, but I will do you justice if ever I reach England".

These events must have been overwhelming for Bligh, especially when the *Bounty* sailed away and left them alone in the vastness of the Pacific Ocean, and he later wrote in his journal that:

> I can only conjecture that they have ideally assured themselves of a more happy life among the Otaheiteans than they could possibly have in England, which joined to some female connections has most likely been the leading cause of the whole business.

The first consideration Lieutenant Bligh and his companions had regarding being cast adrift in their open boat was to examine their resources. Fortunately, Bligh had a compass, a sextant, a quadrant, and a book of nautical tables by which longitude could be calculated that John Samuel probably obtained from his cabin. A pocket watch had been fortuitously carried on board by William Peckover, and Thomas Hayward, a midshipman, had a leather-bound signal book, small enough to fit into a man's pocket but with blank pages that would allow Bligh to keep a record of their voyage and fill with latitudes, estimates of longitudes, compass points, wind directions and details of the uncharted waters they would encounter. They had carpenter Purcell's tools and a copper pot, and the drawing above shows Bligh being tossed one of four cutlasses.

The second consideration was where they could go. For Bligh, there was only one option. The Dutch port of Kupang, at the westernmost point of the island of Timor, was the nearest port at which they could get some assistance from any European compatriots. If Bligh could reach Kupang, the commission secured by John Samuel would prove his command rather than them being regarded with suspicion as mutineers. However, there was another option because Bligh knew that more than six months before he departed from England, a fleet of eleven ships had left on 13 May 1787 carrying 1400 convicts, marines, seamen and civil officers to establish a convict colony at Botany Bay on the east coast of Australia. However, he did not know the success of the proposed colony.

The number of provisions they found to have been thrown into the boat amounted to one hundred and fifty pounds of bread, sixteen pieces of pork, each weighing two pounds, six quarts of rum, six bottles of wine, twenty-eight gallons of water, and four empty barrels. The food would have to be carefully rationed, and Bligh created a set of scales from two halves of a coconut shell, some twine, and a piece of dowl. Each evening meal would consist of half a tin cup of water and an amount of bread and pork equal to the weight of one musket ball. They could hardly taste the small portion of pork before it was gone, and the bread was already stale and mouldy.

Ahead of them was a 6700-kilometre journey in the ship's launch, which was only big enough for half the occupants to lay down and rest at any one time. Built with double-diagonal planking, it would become the most famous open boat in maritime history, and according to Bligh:

> We bore away, across a sea where the navigation is but little known, in a small boat twenty-three feet long from stem to stern, deeply laden with eighteen men. I was happy, however, to see that everyone seemed better satisfied with our situation than myself. We bore away under a reefed lug-foresail and having divided the people into watches, and got the boat into a little order, we returned thanks to God for our miraculous preservation, and, in full confidence of His gracious support, I found my mind more at ease than it had been for some time past.

William Bligh was still in command, even if it was only of the ship's launch, and was determined to reach Timor and Kupang so as to bring the mutineers to justice. It is ironic that the personal qualities that so disadvantaged him as captain of the *Bounty* now proved to be invaluable in preserving his and his men's lives, as survival in the open boat now called for iron discipline, superior seamanship and frugality - qualities that William Bligh possessed in abundance.

The nearest island was Tofoa, and they landed there in search of water, coconuts and other food supplies. Here, the natives observed they had no firearms, and Bligh sensed the possibility of an attack as the warriors began clacking together the stones they held firmly in their hands. Ten years earlier, Bligh witnessed the killing of Captain Cook by Hawaiian natives, who had circled menacingly, clacking stones, just like the emerging situation on Tofoa. He and his crew only just managed to get their boat away, but the result was the death of the Quartermaster, John Norton, who was killed on the beach as he freed the launch's stern line. Because of these events, they were afraid to stop and search for food on other islands, especially in Fiji, because these islanders were reputed to kill and eat trespassers.

The long voyage across the Pacific meant days in an open boat under the heat of the tropical sun, which would have blistered their skin, dehydrated their bodies and made their hunger and suffering unbearable. Fortunately, the weather favoured them. Ever since passing Fiji, they'd had nothing but foul weather. Sometimes, it rained all day, drenching the men and almost swamping the boat. This rain and the water they collected saved them because it takes six weeks to die of hunger but only three days for the beginning of organ failure when the body is without water.

Bligh had no charts and only his memory of Cook's charts of the southwest Pacific to go on, but using an improvised log line for distance travelled, his sextant and his nautical almanac, he then managed to plot latitude and longitude and set a reasonably accurate course. Their voyage took them north of Vanuatu, and Bligh knew that it was from there that Luis Vas de Torres ultimately found his way through the Torres Strait.

William Bligh had sailed with James Cook as Master of the *Resolution* on the Captain's third and fateful voyage and learnt his navigational skills under the tutelage of Captain Cook. Their westward course would eventually bring them to the dangers of the Barrier Reef and Bligh now had to remember Cook's map and the location of his Providential Channel, which would allow them to pass safely through the Barrier and into what Cook called the Labyrinth. Eventually, there were signs they were nearing land; occasionally, a seabird happened to land on the yardarm and was captured by a quick-witted seaman, his weak, shaking body suddenly energised by the sight of food. On the night of the 28th of May, the person at the helm heard the sound of breakers. In the moonlight, he could see the white of the breakers directly ahead, and they quickly turned to port and lowered the mainsail. They had arrived at the Barrier Reef. The sea broke furiously over the reef, but in daylight, a break in the reef was discovered, which was some thirty kilometres south of Cook's Providential Channel. The launch rapidly passed through the channel, into smooth water with land in sight, and all their past hardships were temporarily forgotten. Later, in a letter to Joseph Banks, Bligh describes the midnight arrival:

> At 1 a.m., I fell in with the most dreadful breakers, but I was able to stand clear of them. I stood, however, all night to the NNE and, at daylight, steered in to determine whether the reef was detached or part of the Main Reef. At 9 a.m., I made the Main Reef and discovered an opening half a mile wide with a strong current setting west… deep water in the channel.

They had traversed what became known as the Bligh Boat Channel, and on the evening of 29 May 1789, they landed on the sandy point of an island just off the mainland. A party sent out to reconnoitre rejoiced at finding plenty of oysters on the rocks. With the help of a small magnifying—glass, they lit a fire, and a mixture of oysters, bread, and the last of their pork went into the copper pot to make a stew. Each person received a full pint and had a full stomach for the first time in many weeks. Another luxury was to stretch out on solid ground without being cramped by other bodies. Bligh wrote:

> This day being the anniversary of the Restoration of King Charles II, and the name not being inapplicable to our present situation (for we were restored to fresh life and strength), I named this Restoration Island.

Their sojourn on the island only lasted two days, but Bligh believed it saved their lives and helped sustain them for the rest of the voyage. Before their departure, they prayed to thank God for having safely crossed the Pacific, passed through the Barrier Reef, and reached the Australian mainland. Bligh tried to remember a common prayer and wrote in his notebook what has become known as Bligh's Prayer:

> O' Lord our Heavenly Father, Almighty and everlasting God, who has safely brought us to the beginning of this day; In and through the merits of our blessed Saviour through whom we are taught to ask all things, - We thy unworthy servants prostrate ourselves before thee and humbly ask forgiveness of our sins and transgressions. We most devoutly thank thee for our preservation and are truly conscious that it is only through thy Divine Mercy we have been saved.

Bligh was now safely inside the Great Barrier Reef and had to recall by memory the chart James Cook made almost twenty years earlier. He described the coast as they approached Cape York and the Torres Strait.

> June 3. the coast has the appearance of a sandy desert, but improves about three leagues farther to the northward, where it terminates in a point, near to which is a number of small islands. I sailed between these islands, (Adolphus Channel) where

> I found bottom at twelve fathoms; the high mountainous island with a flat top (Mount Adolphus) and four rocks to the S E of it, that I called the Brothers, being on my starboard hand. Soon after, an extensive opening appeared in the mainland, with several high islands in it. I called this the Bay of Islands. I have little doubt that the opening I have named the Bay of Islands is Endeavour Strait.

Bligh continued to sail to the northwest, they passed to the north of the Prince of Wales group of islands, naming one of them Wednesday Island (Maururra), and left the Torres Strait through what was to become known as the Prince of Wales Channel:

> June 4. The coast to the northward and westward of the Bay of Islands had a very different appearance from that to the southward. It was high and woody, with many islands close to it, and had a very broken appearance. Among these islands are fine bays, and convenient places for shipping. The northernmost I call Wednesday Island: to the N W of this we fell in with a large reef, which I believe joins a number of cays that were in sight from the N W to the E N E. We now stood to the S W half a league, when it was noon, and I had a good observation of the latitude in 10° 31′ S. I now assured everyone that we should be clear of New Holland in the afternoon ... At eight o'clock in the evening, we once more launched into the open ocean. Miserable as our situation was in every respect, I was secretly surprised to see that it did not appear to affect anyone so strongly as myself; on the contrary, it seemed as if they had embarked on a voyage to Timor, in a vessel sufficiently calculated for safety and convenience.

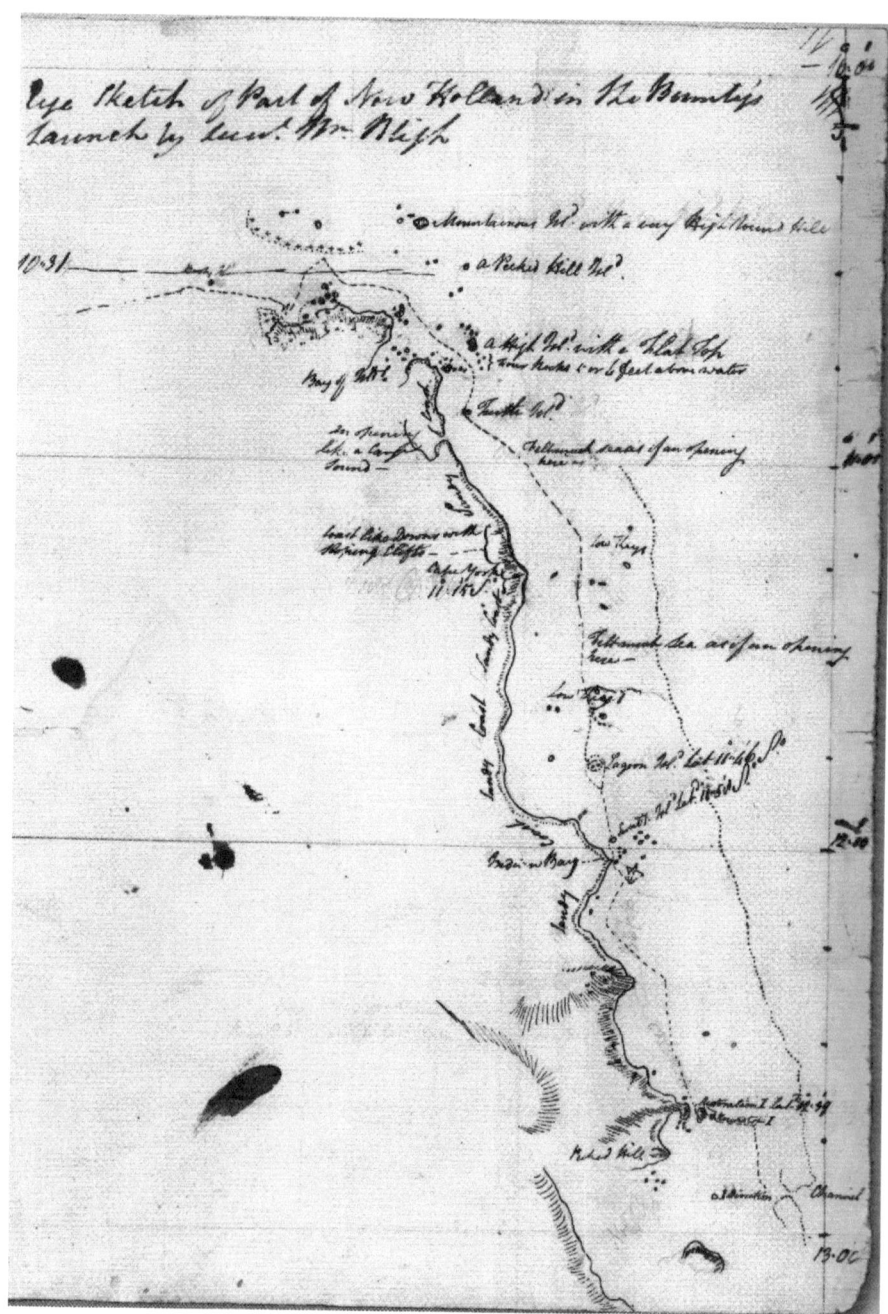

Sketch of part of New Holland
William Bligh, 1789, State Library NSW

The Sketch shows the voyage of the *Bounty*'s launch from Restoration Island through the Torres Strait to Booby Island. Bligh was proud of his running survey of the northeast coast of New Holland and Torres Strait, as he carried out complex nautical calculations in a situation of great distress. Others later realised Bligh's appraisal of his own chart was justified, and Mathew Flinders expressed his high regard for Bligh's cartography:

> It has been to me a cause of much surprise that under such distress of hunger and fatigue, and of anxiety still greater than these, and whilst running before a strong breeze in an open boat, Captain Bligh should have been able to gather materials for a chart; but that this chart should possess a considerable share of accuracy, is a subject for admiration.

Conscious of the deteriorating health of the crew, Bligh increased their ration of bread to three times a day instead of the usual two times. He could see from the traces of rockweed drifting past and from the increasing numbers of seabirds that he was close to land, but the worsening condition of the men around him caused him concern:

> An extreme weakness, swelled legs, hollow and ghastly countenances, great propensity to sleep and an apparent debility of understanding, gave me melancholy proofs of an approaching dissolution of my people.

This was Bligh's darkest hour. He stood to lose everything if he did not find a safe harbour. The loss of the *Bounty* was a disaster, but his navigational skills and fierce determination to bring the mutineers to justice would deliver them to safety. He must have been praying they could complete their voyage, and fortunately, at about three o'clock in the morning, the shapeless silhouette of the island of Timor emerged out of the darkness. They had crossed 6700 kilometres of open sea, enduring native attack, storms, hunger and despair, but had survived, and Bligh wrote:

> June 12. It is not possible for me to describe the pleasure which the blessing of the sight of this land diffused among us. It appeared scarcely credible to ourselves that, in an open boat, and so poorly provided, we should have been able to reach the coast of Timor in forty-one days after leaving Tofoa, having in that time run, by our log, a distance of three thousand six hundred and eighteen nautical miles; and that, notwithstanding our extreme distress, no one should have perished in the voyage.

Arriving in Kupang Bay, Bligh describes the desperate condition of himself and his men and the reaction of the people of Timor who met them on the beach:

> June 14. An indifferent spectator (if such could be found) would have been at a loss which most to admire, the eyes of famine sparkling at immediate relief, or the horror of their preservers at the sight of so many spectres, whose ghastly countenances, if the cause had been unknown, would rather have excited terror than pity. Our bodies were nothing but skin and bones, our limbs were full of sores, and we were clothed in rags, in this condition, with the tears of joy and gratitude flowing down our cheeks, the people of Timor beheld us with a mixture of horror, surprise and pity.

It was William Bligh's determination to follow standard naval procedures and routines that helped keep order and sanity amongst the crew, which enabled the launch to reach Timor safely. Their assigned tasks included manning the tiller, bailing water, working the sails, and working the log line, which involved one man counting the seconds and another counting the knots as the log line was reeled in. Bligh's iron will and his implementation of naval routine, coupled with his seamanship, saved them. On the rare occasions when the group reached land, conflict broke out, but at sea, Bligh was unquestionably the master of his crew. At the most fundamental level, the crew trusted him as an excellent navigator whose skills would bring them to safety. Unfortunately, they did not all survive the voyage, and within days of reaching Timor, David Nelson, the botanist, died. Bligh wrote of his most reliable friend:

> The loss of this honest man bears very heavy on my mind, his duty and integrity went hand in hand, and he accomplished through great care and diligence the object he was sent out for.

Bligh obtained passage from Kupang to Batavia and found a berth on a Dutch ship sailing for Holland. He arrived in England on 14 March 1790 and became an almost instant hero. To have survived the voyage in the launch and returned safely to his homeland was reason enough for his status. He rapidly published an account of the mutiny and their open boat voyage as part of a campaign to secure his position. Since he was the first to return, he had the advantage of complete control of the story about the mutiny and his subsequent tribulations. Because of their extreme privations, only twelve of the eighteen crew cast off in the launch with Bligh survived to return to England; these crewmen arrived back over the next few months, and some of them had a different story to tell.

8

The Search for the Bounty Mutineers, 1791

> Never fear my boys, we'll all go to hell together.
>
> John Grimwood, Master-at-arms, *HMS Pandora*.

In accordance with Naval Law, William Bligh faced a court-martial for the loss of His Majesty's Armed Vessel *Bounty*. In October 1790, he was honourably acquitted, and shortly thereafter, he published - *A Narrative of the Mutiny on board His Majesty's Ship Bounty; And the Subsequent Voyage of Part of the Crew, in the Ship's Boat, from Tofoa, one of the Friendly Islands, to Timor, a Dutch Settlement in the East Indies*. The publication of Bligh's account of the voyage to Timor and his sufferings excited the strongest public interest and sympathy.

The Admiralty immediately decided to send a ship to capture the mutineers and return them to England for a court martial. For this purpose, *HMS Pandora*, a frigate of twenty-four guns with one hundred and thirty men on board, was despatched under the command of Captain Edward Edwards with orders to proceed to Tahiti. The Admiralty ordered the doubling of the usual number of masters' mates and midshipmen for this voyage in the event the *HMS Bounty* was retaken and could be brought back to Britain.

Captain Edward Edwards, the officer chosen for the command, had a high reputation as a seaman and a strict disciplinarian. Since the Admiralty saw this voyage as a police mission, no better choice could have been made. The crew was largely composed of new recruits, for every trained seaman in the navy had gone to man the vessels of the fleet being assembled at Portsmouth to participate in what became the Battle of Ushant or the 'Battle of the Glorious First of June' against the French Republic. Many of these new recruits had been drawn into service by being offered a bonus and two months of advance pay.

The Admiralty issued the *Pandora's* sailing instructions on 25 October 1790. After reaching Tahiti, Captain Edwards was to search the different groups of the Society and Friendly Islands to capture the mutineers and bring them back for trial:

> You are to keep the Mutineers as closely confined as may preclude all possibility of them escaping, having, however, proper regard for the preservation of their lives, that they may be brought home to undergo the punishment due to their demerits.

Thomas Hayward, one of the *Bounty's* former midshipmen, who had survived the open boat voyage to Timor, was among the junior officers added to *Pandora's* complement. Hayward's participation in the search would assist Captain Edwards in recognising the mutineers. He could also act as an interpreter in the contacts and interviews they would have with local chiefs.

The *Pandora* sailed from The Solent on 7 November 1790 and, after an uneventful voyage around Cape Horn, arrived at Tahiti on 23 March 1791. Shortly after their arrival, four of the mutineers surrendered to Captain Edwards. These were Joseph Coleman, the *Bounty's* armourer, midshipmen Peter Heyward, George Stewart and able seaman Richard Skinner. Edwards then dispatched search parties to round up the remainder of those living on Tahiti; James Morrison, Charles Norman and Thomas Ellison, who had tried to build an escape boat, were eventually captured and brought back to the *Pandora*. The half-blind Michael Byrne, who had been fiddler aboard *Bounty*, had also come aboard by this time. Edwards conducted further searches over the next few weeks, and Henry Hilbrant and Thomas McIntosh were captured and brought aboard the *Pandora*.

We have not learnt of the obligations of Captain Edwards, but *Pandora's* surgeon, George Hamilton, describes Tahitian customs and his responsibility as a senior member of His Majesty's Royal Navy:

> In becoming the Tyo, or friend of a man, it is expected you pay him a compliment, by cherishing his wife; but, being ignorant of that ceremony, I very innocently gave high offence to Matuara, the king of York Island, to whom I was introduced as his friend: a shyness took place on the side of his Majesty, from my neglect to his wife; but, through the medium of Brown the interpreter, he put me in mind of my duty, and on my promising my endeavours, matters were for that time made up. It was to me, however, a very serious inauguration: I was, in the first place, not a young man, and had been onshore a whole week; the lady was a woman of rank, being sister to Ottoo, the king of Otaheitee, and had in her youth been beautiful, and named Peggy Ottoo. But Peggy had seen much service and bore away many honourable scars in the fields of Venus. However, his Majesty's service must be done, and Matuara and I were again friends.

By 9 April 1791, fourteen of the mutineers had been apprehended and locked up in a wooden prison cell built on the quarterdeck, which came to be referred to as 'Pandora's Box'. An armed guard consisting of two marines and a midshipman was posted around the clock to ensure that the prisoners were isolated and did not communicate with the crew. The prisoners were interrogated, and Edwards learned that after the mutiny, the *Bounty* had sailed to Tubuai in present-day French Polynesia, approximately 330 kilometres south of Tahiti. An attempt to establish a settlement there failed after the excessive brutality and violence directed against those natives resisting Christian's attempt to colonise their island. The *Bounty* then sailed back to Tahiti, where sixteen of the mutineers were put ashore at their own request; the remaining nine decided they were already dead men if captured by the British Navy and chose to continue in the *Bounty* to an undisclosed location.

Pitcairn Island had been sighted on 3 July 1767 by the crew of the British sloop *HMS Swallow*, commanded by Captain Philip Carteret. His measurement of its longitude was incorrect, which made the island difficult to find as he had placed it 330 kilometres to the west of its actual location, as highlighted by the failure of Captain James Cook to locate the island in July 1773. For Fletcher Christian and his fellow mutineers, the difficulty in locating this island made it an ideal location to hide from what they knew would be an extensive search by the British Navy.

On the night of the 21st of September, the *Bounty* sailed from Tahiti with nine mutineers, seven Tahitian men and fourteen women onboard and was last seen the following morning to the northwest of Point Venus. In his narrative, George Hamilton gives us his description of the mutiny, Fletcher Christian, and the possibility of a future British colony in the South Seas:

> That unfortunate man Christian has, in a rash unguarded moment, been tempted to swerve from his duty to his king and country. As he is in other respects of an amiable character and respectable abilities, should he elude the hand of justice, it may be hoped he will employ his talents in humanising the rude savages; so that, at some future period, a British lion may blaze forth in the south with all the characteristic virtues of the English nation, and complete the great prophecy, by propagating the Christian knowledge amongst the infidels. As Christian has taken fourteen beautiful women with him from Otaheite,

there is little doubt of his intention of colonising some undiscovered island.

True to his promise, William Bligh had written to the Admiralty from Kupang in August 1779, after his open boat voyage, stating that Joseph Coleman, Michel Byrne, Thomas McIntosh and Charles Norman had been kept onboard against their wishes and deserved mercy. However, they weren't shown any mercy by Captain Edwards; for him, the different parts played by these men in the mutiny were irrelevant. He had his orders, and for him, all fourteen men would be considered equally guilty until they could be tried and sentenced in England. For a period, the prisoners' Tahitian wives were allowed to visit the ship and bring their children. As described by George Hamilton:

> Their wives brought them ample supplies of every delicacy that the country afforded and behaved with the greatest fidelity and affection to them. To see the poor captives in irons weeping over their tender offspring was too moving a scene for any feeling heart and Captain Edwards had to ban any further visits.

Leaving Tahiti on 8 May 1791, the *Pandora* searched for the *Bounty* and the remaining mutineers for the next four months. As they sailed westward, the search took them to Tokelau, Samoa, Niue and the Ha'apai Islands, without any sighting of the *Bounty* mutineers and taking the *Pandora* further away from Pitcairn Island. When passing the island of Vanikoro on 13 August 1791, they observed smoke signals rising from the island. Edwards, single-minded in his search for the *Bounty* and convinced that mutineers fearful of discovery would not be advertising their whereabouts, ignored the smoke signals and sailed on. Sven Wahlroos, in his 1989 book *Mutiny and Romance in the South Seas*, argues that the smoke signals were a distress message sent by survivors of the Lapérouse expedition, which later evidence indicated were still alive on Vanikoro three years after their vessels had foundered. Wahlroos is 'virtually certain' that Captain Edwards missed his chance to become 'one of the heroes of maritime history' by solving the mystery of the lost Lapérouse expedition.

On reaching the Tongan Islands we have one of George Hamilton's descriptions of the indiscretions in which he and his companions were engaged:

> On the 29th, we anchored in the road of Anamooka. Immediately on our arrival, a large sailing canoe was hired, and Lieut. Hayward and one private sent to the Happai and Feegee Islands, to make inquiry after the *Bounty* but received no intelligence.
>
> The women here are extremely beautiful; and although they want that feminine softness of manners which the Otaheite women possess in so eminent a degree, their matchless vivacity, and fine animated countenances, compensate the want of the softer blandishments of their sister island.
>
> Many beautiful girls were brought on board for sale by their mothers, who were very exorbitant in their demands, as nothing less than a broad axe would satisfy them; but after standing their market three days, *la pucelage* fell to an old razor, a pair of scissors, or a very large nail. Indeed, this trade was pushed to so great a height, that the quarter-deck became the scene of the most indelicate familiarities. Nor did the unfeeling mothers commiserate with the pain and suffering of the poor girls but seemed to enjoy it as a monstrous good thing. It is customary here, when girls meet with an accident of this kind, that a council of matrons is held, and the noviciate has a gash made in her forefinger. We soon observed a number of cut fingers amongst them; and had the razors held out, I believe all the girls on the island would have undergone the same operation.

Because of these descriptions, George Hamilton was later branded as 'a course, vulgar, and illiterate man, more disposed to relate licentious scenes and adventures, in which he and his companions were engaged than to give any information of proceedings and occurrences connected with the main object of the voyage'.

On 26 August 1791, the *Pandora* first sighted the Barrier Reef. Edwards could have decided to follow the passages discovered by Cook and Bligh but sailed further north to find a more direct route through the Reef and into the Torres Strait. Late in the afternoon of 28 August, *Pandora's* lookout saw what looked like a volcanic island and an entrance through the reef. Lieutenant Corner was sent in the yawl to investigate while the *Pandora* moved to deep water. As described by George Hamilton:

> We stood to the westward, where there appeared to be an opening. We saw an island in that direction, and a reef extending a considerable way to the northwest. Hauled upon the wind, seeing our passage obstructed, and stood off under an easy sail in the night, till daylight; and in the morning bore away, and discovered four islands, to which the name of Murray's Islands was given … We kept running along the reef, and in the forenoon thought we saw an opening. Lieut. Corner was immediately ordered to get ready, to discover if there was a passage for the ship, and went to the top masthead, to look well around him before he left us.

At 5 pm, Lieutenant Corner on the yawl signalled there was indeed a passage fit for the ship and started to return. The yawl made slow progress in beating back to the windward against the tide, which was now pouring into the reef passage at an estimated rate of 10 knots. It was getting dark and the crew feared they would lose him in the night. As this drama played out and the crew focused on the yawl, the *Pandora* drifted towards the Barrier Reef. Corner eventually brought the yawl up to the frigate's stern, but before it was on board, the current slammed the *Pandora* onto the Reef with such force that the rudder and part of the sternpost were broken away.

H M Ship Pandora in the act of Foundering
Lt-Col Robert Batty, 1831, State Library NSW

The carpenter reported that *Pandora* made eighteen inches of water in five minutes and had been the same in another five minutes after this. The crew turned to the pumps and to bail, but the water gained so quickly that there were eight feet in the hold in little more than an hour and a half after she struck. Shortly before dawn, the Captain and officers conferred on the quarterdeck. They agreed that nothing could be done to save the ship as the water was now coming in faster at the gun ports than the pumps could discharge; the order was given to abandon the ship and release the prisoners. The ship's boats, consisting of one launch, one eight-oared pinnace and two six-oared yawls, were kept astern of the ship, and a quantity of bread, water, and other necessary articles were put into them. The image shows the crew abandoning the ship and those that could swim trying to reach the ship's boats, which were astern. According to Captain Edwards's report:

> Scarcely was this affected when the ship went down, leaving nothing visible but the top-mast cross-trees. The master-at-arms and all the sentinels sunk with the ship. The cries of

them and the other drowning men were awful in the extreme; and more than half an hour elapsed before the survivors could be taken up by the boats.

In the hours after the wreck, the ship's boats reached a sandy cay about six kilometres distant. On mustering those saved, it was found that eighty-nine of *Pandora's* crew survived the wreck, and thirty-one had drowned. Of the prisoners, ten survived, and the remaining four were unable to escape from Pandora's Box before the ship finally sunk.

According to Hamilton's account, the ship suddenly heeled over and began to sink before all the prisoners could be unchained and let out of Pandora's Box. Fortunately, John Grimwood, the master-at-arms, let the keys of their irons fall through the entrance, which he had just opened, crying, "Never fear my boys, we'll all go to hell together". This enabled them to commence their own escape in which they were assisted, at the imminent risk of his own life, by William Moulter, a boatswain's mate, saying he would set them free or go to the bottom with them. Moulter's humanitarian deed was recognised in 1984 when the cay at the eastern side of Pandora's Entrance, referred to as Entrance Cay, was officially renamed Moulter Cay.

During the two days the survivors spent on Entrance Cay, several of them were involved in making the four boats more seaworthy by breaking up the boats' floors and using them and spare canvas to raise their freeboard to prevent water coming in over the bows of the heavily laden boats. From the report of Captain Edwards:

> August 31st. The boats were completed and were launched, and we put everything we had saved on board of them and at half past ten in the forenoon we embarked, 30 on board the launch, 25 in the pinnace, 23 in one yawl and 21 in the other yawl. We steered N.W. by W. and W.N.W. within the reef. This channel through the reef is better than any hitherto known, besides the advantage it has of being situated further to the

North, by which many difficulties would be avoided when within the reef.

They sighted Cape York in the morning and steered towards Adolphus Island where Islanders helped them fill their water barrels:

> September 1. I steered for an island called by Lt. Bligh, Mountainous Island (Adolphus Island), and when joined by the boats ran into a bay of that island where we saw Indians on the beach. The water was shoal and the Indians waded off to the boats. I gave them some presents and made them sensible that we were in want of water. They brought us a vessel filled with water which we had given them for the purpose, and they returned to fill it again. They used many signs to signify that they wished us to land, but we declined their invitation from motives of prudence.

Edwards and his fleet of small boats then sailed north-westwards and found a sheltered anchorage near Wednesday Island. They came ashore to gorge themselves on the wongai plum that grows there, and the party camped on the north coast of Prince of Wales Island (Muralug), where the men were upset at night by the howling of 'wolves', possibly dingoes, and Edwards named it Wolves Bay. He and his men also noted how a gravesite at Wolves Bay had been decorated with dugong and turtle bones, two human skulls and a long wooden paddle.

> September 2. In the evening we saw the Northernmost Extremity of New South Wales, which forms the South side of Endeavour Straits. At night the boats took each other in tow and we steered to the Westward.
>
> It is unnecessary to detail our particular sufferings in the boats during our run to Timor and it is sufficient to observe that we suffered more from heat and thirst than from hunger, and that our strength was greatly decreased. We fortunately

had good weather, the sea was generally not very rough, and the boats were more buoyant and livelier in the water than we reasonably could have expected considering the weight and numbers we had in them.

This was the second time in as many years that midshipman Thomas Hayward had to cross the Torres Strait in a desperate voyage to reach safety, and he must have sworn this was the last time he had ever wanted to see this part of the world. Favoured by a fair wind and a calm sea, Edwards's small fleet of boats made the run to Timor in twelve days. Like Bligh, he found that the young bore their privations better than the old and that the first effect of thirst and famine is to make men excessively irritable. On the open boat voyage, the irrepressible George Hamilton records an incident regarding his captain. Edwards neglected to conduct Sunday prayers until he was reminded of his duty when one of the mutineers led the devotions in the boat's bow. Scandalised at the impropriety of a mutineer daring to appeal to the Highest Tribunal for mercy and behind the back of the earthly court before which he was due to be arraigned, Captain Edwards sternly reproved him and continued the prayers himself.

Timor was sighted on 13 September 1791, fifteen days after the wreck of the *Pandora*, and the launch and pinnace reached the Dutch East India Company's fort at Kupang on 16 September. According to Edwards, nothing could exceed the kindness and hospitality of the governor and other Dutch officers of this settlement in offering every possible assistance and relief to their distressed condition.

The group sailed from Kupang on a Dutch vessel and arrived in Batavia on the 7th of November. Hamilton describes how their first care was to get the sick members of the crew to hospital, 'However, some dead bodies floating down the canal struck our boat, which had a very disagreeable effect on the minds of our brave fellows, whose nerves were reduced to a very weak state from sickness'. The Dutch East India Company offered to divide the group among four ships proceeding to Holland. Captain Edwards took the prisoners with him in the *Vreedenburgh*, but finding his Majesty's ship Gorgon at the Cape of Good Hope, he transhipped himself and his prisoners and proceeded to Spithead, where they arrived on the 19th of June, 1792.

The trials of the ten surviving *Bounty* mutineers were held in September 1792. As hoped, the four crewmen who could not join Bligh in the longboat, Joseph Coleman, Michael Byrne, Thomas McIntosh and Charles Norman, were acquitted. Thomas Ellison, John Millward, Thomas Burkitt and William Muspratt – were all found guilty of mutiny for which there was a mandatory death sentence. However, only Ellison, Millward and Burkitt were hung. Muspratt appealed and was acquitted on a legal technicality nearly one year later. The court recommended James Morrison and Peter Heywood to the King's mercy, whereupon they eventually received a Royal pardon. They are reported to have received the news of their pardon 'with a flood of tears upon which, having been reminded of the shamefulness of their actions during the mutiny, they swore eternal devotion to duty and gratitude to their monarch for his goodwill towards them'.

Contradictory statements and possible false testimony clouded the extent of Heywood's true guilt in the mutiny. During his trial, powerful family connections worked on his behalf, and he also benefited from the Fletcher Christian family's efforts to demean Bligh's character and present the mutiny as an understandable reaction to unbearable tyranny. Contemporary press reports contrasted Heywood's pardon with the fate of those who were hanged, who were all lower-deck sailors without wealth, family influence and legal counsel. Peter Heywood was able to resume his naval career and eventually retired with the rank of post-captain.

In 1791, another open boat arrived in Kupang after a desperate voyage to safety. It included eight men, one woman and two children, claiming to be survivors of another English vessel shipwrecked on the Barrier Reef.

9

Escape from Port Jackson, 1791

> I confess that I never looked at these people without pity and astonishment. They had miscarried in a heroic struggle for liberty after having combated every hardship and conquered every difficulty.
>
> Watkin Tench, Captain Lieutenant, Royal Marines

The First Fleet departed from Portsmouth on 13 May 1787 and was comprised of six convict transports, two Royal Navy warships and three store ships. The convict ships were the *Alexander*, the *Charlotte*, the *Friendship*, the *Lady Penrhyn*, the *Prince of Wales* and the *Scarborough*. The Royal Navy escorts were HMS *Sirius* and HMS *Supply*, and the store ships were *Golden Grove*, *Fishburn* and *Borrowdale*. Aboard the fleet were approximately 210 officers and marines (some with their families) and around 775 convicts, including 582 men and 193 women. The convicts had committed a variety of crimes, including theft, perjury, fraud, assault and robbery, for which they had variously been sentenced to penal transportation for 7 years, 14 years, or, in the worst cases, for the term of their natural life.

All the ships of the Fleet had arrived in Botany Bay by 21 January 1788, but despite the descriptions of Cook and Banks, the site was found unsuitable for a colony, and they moved to Sydney Cove on 26 January. Watkin Tench, the Captain of the Marines who sailed on the *Charlotte*, describes the first days of the settlement, which involved clearing trees and setting up a campsite:

> For the purpose of expediting the public work, the male convicts have been divided into gangs, over each of which a person, selected from among themselves, is placed. It is to be regretted that Government did not take this matter into consideration before we left England and appoint proper persons with reasonable salaries to execute the office of overseers; as the consequence of our present imperfect plan is such, as to defeat in a great measure the purposes for which the prisoners were sent out. The female convicts have hitherto lived in a state of total idleness; except a few who are kept at work in making pegs for tiles and picking up shells for burning into lime. For the last time I repeat, that the behaviour of all classes of these people since our arrival in the settlement has been better than could, I think, have been expected from them.

Food was scarce in the colony's early years, and William Bryant's seamanship and fishing skills, which he had learnt in his native Cornwall, saw him placed in charge of managing the colony's fishing enterprise. Bryant's role gave him and his family a relatively privileged position. William Bryant and Mary Broad had sailed on the convict ship *Charlotte*, named their first-born child Charlotte, and subsequently married in the colony. The harbour fish included bass, mullet, skate, sole, leatherjacket and another species, which they named the light-horseman. This was a job of particular importance when, in April 1790, all were placed upon a subsistence ration. Bryant was also allowed to keep some of his catch by way of an incentive, but he was caught abusing this privilege, and on 4 February 1789, he was charged with 'secreting and selling large quantities of fish'. The main witness for the prosecution was the convict Joseph Paget, who worked in Bryant's fishing boat and acted as an intermediary to pass on fish in exchange for spirits or other goods.

Captain Hunter was ordered to sail the *Sirius* to the Cape of Good Hope for emergency supplies in October 1788. Following the southerly winds, he sailed eastward towards Cape Horn and then to Capetown. From there, he returned to Sydney Cove, arriving in May 1789 and thus circumnavigating the globe. The voyage was made more difficult by the leaky state of the ship, which rendered continual pumping necessary. *Sirius* was then refitted and sent to Norfolk Island with a large party of convicts but was caught in a violent storm and wrecked after being driven onto a coral reef.

In 1790, with the colony again desperate for food, Lieutenant Henry Ball with the *Supply* was sent to Batavia and returned laden with foodstuffs. His voyage on what was the safest route, around the north coast of New Guinea, took the little ship six months to complete. In Batavia, he commissioned a Dutch East India Company vessel, the *Waaksamheyd*, under the command of Captain Detmar Smit to bring 171 barrels of beef, 172 barrels of pork, 39 barrels of flour, 1000 pounds of sugar and 70,000 pounds of rice to Port Jackson by way of the north coast of New Guinea.

William Bryant had hatched a plan to escape from the convict colony and began to collect the necessary equipment and supplies. It is thought that Mary Bryant found means to persuade Detmar Smit with liquor, money, or personal services to provide a quadrant, a compass, a chart and information about the voyage north, two muskets, a small quantity of powder and some lead shot. For supplies, the group had 100 pounds of rice, 14 pounds of pork obtained from Smit and 100 pounds of flour obtained illegally from the colony baker. To supply themselves with water, they obtained eight casks. Bryant and company dug out cavities underneath his hut's floorboards to store their acquired equipment. In addition, they stockpiled other goods, with Private John Easty reporting that they gathered 'a large quantity of equipment of all sorts for providing the boat with beds, bedding, sails, firearms and ammunition, plus material to effect repairs to the boat when needed and a fishing net'.

The escapees were William Bryant, his wife Mary Bryant, and their two young children — Charlotte, a three-year-old girl, and Emanuel, a one-year-old boy. William Morton, the boat's navigator; James Martin, the chronicler of their voyage, with James Cox, Samuel Bird, William Allen, Samuel Broom, and Nathaniel Lilley.

William Bryant was a fisherman and smuggler from Cornwall who had been arrested for resisting revenue officers who attempted to seize some smuggled goods in his possession. Bryant was convicted at the Cornwall Assizes of 20 March 1784 and sentenced to death, subsequently commuted on condition of his being transported for seven years.

Mary Bryant grew up in Cornwall as the daughter of a fisherman. Together with Catherine Prior and Mary Hayden, she was convicted of robbing and violently assaulting Agnes Lakeman on a road in Plymouth. They stole a silk bonnet valued at 12 pence and other goods valued at £1 and 11 shillings. All three were condemned to death, but this sentence was commuted to transportation for seven years. Mary gave birth to her daughter, Charlotte, aboard the convict vessel *Charlotte* in the Southern Ocean.

William Morton, the navigator of the escapees' boat, was perhaps the group's most important member. An experienced seaman, he was convicted of obtaining money by false pretences at the Newcastle-upon-Tyne Quarter Sessions on 24 April 1789 and sentenced to seven years of transportation.

William Allen was also an experienced sailor, having served in the Royal Navy, the North American Squadron and merchant ships. Allen was convicted of stealing 49 linen handkerchiefs valued at 35 shillings and was sentenced to seven years of transportation.

Samuel Broom (alias John Butcher) was a farm labourer who was convicted at the Shropshire Assizes on 26 July 1788 of stealing three pigs from John Harsbury and sentenced to seven years of transportation.

James Cox was indicted for breaking and entering the dwelling-house of Henry and Francis Thompson, haberdashers on Oxford Street, London, and for stealing 12 yards of thread lace valued at £4 and two pairs of cotton stockings valued at four shillings.

Samuel Bird was employed as a waterman and sentenced to transportation for seven years at the Surrey Assizes on 20 July 1785 for stealing 1000lbs (453 kg) of saltpetre from a warehouse in Wandsworth.

Nathaniel Lilley, a weaver by trade, was convicted at the Suffolk Assizes on 19 March 1788 and sentenced to death. He was subsequently commuted to transportation for the term of his natural life for the burglary of the house of a baker in Sudbury, from which he took, among other things, a silver-cased watch, two silver tablespoons, and a fishnet.

James Martin was convicted of stealing iron bolts valued at two shillings and sixpence and lead valued at two shillings. Given that he was a bricklayer and stonemason by trade, it is reasonable to assume this was a workplace theft. Not all of this group would have been literate, but we know that James Martin was because he later wrote the account of their desperate voyage.

William Bryant chose to recruit his crew extremely well. William Morton was an experienced seaman with a knowledge of navigation. Mary Bryant, who grew up in the fishing community of Fowey, could presumably handle a boat, and William Allen was an experienced sailor. James Cox's carpentry skills and Nathaniel Lillie's weaving skills would also have been useful in repairing the boat, sails, and the escapees' clothing.

On 22 March 1791, the *Supply* sailed to the Norfolk Island colony, and six days later, the *Waaksamheyd* also departed Port Jackson, having been chartered to return Captain Hunter and the crew of the *Sirius* to England. Now, no ship in the harbour could outrun the escapees in their launch. Under cover of darkness on the moonless night of 28 March, Bryant and his fellow escapees loaded the six-oared longboat 'the Governor's Cutter' with their supplies and silently rowed their way down the harbour, past the Look-out at South Head and out into the open ocean. It was only the next morning that the escape was discovered. There was a certain amount of sympathy and admiration in the colony for the escapees, and Watkin Tench, a Captain Lieutenant of the Marines, wrote:

> March 1791. The Dutch vessel had just sailed, when a very daring manoeuvre was carried into execution, with complete success, by a set of convicts, eleven in number, including a woman, wife of one of the parties, and two little children. They seized the governor's cutter and putting into her a seine, fishing-lines and hooks, firearms, a quadrant, compass, and some provisions, boldly pushed out to sea, determined to brave every danger and combat every hardship, rather than remain longer in a captive state. Most of these people had been brought out in the First fleet, and the terms of transportation of some of them were expired. Among them were a fisherman, a carpenter, and some competent navigators, so that little doubt was entertained that a scheme so admirably planned would be adequately executed. When their elopement was discovered, a pursuit was ordered by the governor. But the fugitives had made good use of the intermediate time to be no longer seen by their pursuers. After the voyage of Captain Bligh, which was well known to us, no length of passage or hazard of navigation seemed above human accomplishment. However, to prevent future attempts of a like nature, the governor directed those boats only of the stated dimensions should be built.

The escapee's voyage up the east coast of Australia is not well documented but we know that after two days, they landed somewhere south of present-day Newcastle and were the first to discover coal in New South Wales, as James Martin wrote in his chronicle of their escape:

> Walking along the shore towards the entrance of the creek we found several large pieces of coal – seeing so many pieces we

thought it was not unlikely to find a mine, and searching about a little, we found a place where we picked up with an axe as good coals as any in England – we took some to the fire and they burned exceedingly well. The natives came, to whom we gave some clothes and other articles and went away well satisfied.

Needing to collect water and make repairs, they found a harbour, possibly Port Stephens, where they hauled the cutter ashore to repair her seams:

> We rowed up the harbour 9 or 10 miles till we made a little white Sandy Island in the middle of the harbour, which we landed upon and hauled up our boat and repaired her bottom with what little materials we had whilst our stay of 2 days we had no interruption from the Natives — then we rowed off to the main where we took in fresh water and a few Cabbage trees — and then put out to sea.

They then ran into rough weather, with their vessel dangerously overloaded and waves breaking over the boat's sides. This could have been the end of their escape and the end of themselves. They threw some items overboard to lighten their load and then sought shelter close to shore:

> That night we ran into an open bay, but we could see no place to land so that we were afraid of staving our boat to pieces. We came to anchor in the night but about 2 o'clock in the morning our anchor broke and we were drove into the middle of the surf expecting at every moment that our boat would be staved to pieces and every soul perish, but as God would have it we got our boat safe onshore without any loss or damage ... we kindled a fire with great difficulty everything being very wet, we got plenty of shellfish and fresh water.

Further north, near Moreton Bay, they found a suitable landing place with some huts, where they encountered two aboriginal women and their children. They described the two women 'as being frightened and ran away, but we made signs that we wanted a light from their fire-brand, which they gave us but crying at the same time in their way'. The Bryant party spent the night undisturbed in these huts, but the following morning, a great number of aborigines advanced towards the camp, and they were forced to fire a musket over their heads. The next few days were probably the most dangerous of their voyage as they encountered strong winds and such heavy seas that they all expected to drown:

> We were drove out to sea by a heavy gale of wind and current, expecting at every moment to go to the bottom ... the sea coming in so heavy upon us now that two hands were obliged to keep bailing out ... I will leave you to consider what distress we must have been in, the woman and the two little babies were in bad condition, and we had nothing to eat except a little raw rice.

They were able to save themselves by landing on an isolated island on the southern part of the Barrier Reef, which they describe as being only one mile in circumference and populated by large turtles:

> We were rather fearful of going in for fear of staving our boat but we concluded among ourselves that if we kept out to sea we should every soul perish. All around this island there were nothing but reefs but we got in safe without much damage ... We found a great quantity of very fine large turtles which was left upon the reef ... this reef runs about a mile and half out in the sea and is entirely dry when low water. We took and killed one of the turtles and had a noble meal this night. It rained very hard when we spread our mainsail and filled two of our breakers full of water. We stayed on this Island six days during

that time we killed twelve turtles and some of it we took and dried over the fire to take to sea with us

The turtles provided the first fresh meat they had eaten in weeks. With plenty of water, some fresh meat, and no friendly or unfriendly aborigines to disturb them, they stayed here for days collecting and drying turtle meat. The group finally reached Cape York, and hugging the coastline, they entered Torres Strait and its islands. Here, they described the natives they encountered as being 'fatter and blacker than they were in other parts we had seen before'. These, of course, were the Torres Strait Islanders, and 'there was one we took to be the chief as he wore some shells around his shoulders'. According to the group, 'these people seemed to stand in a posture of defence' against the escapees. They resorted to the tried-and-trusted tactic of firing a musket over their heads. However, the islanders stood their ground and returned fire with their bows and arrows, causing the escapees to hoist their sail and depart as quickly as possible.

It is assumed that William Bryant followed Captain Cook's route around Cape York and into the Endeavor Strait before crossing the Gulf of Carpentaria towards Arnhem Land. Here, the escapees describe being chased by a large canoe fitted with matt sails and a platform capable of holding thirty to forty men. These were possibly the Torres Strait Islanders' trading vessels or the Macassans who came to Northern Australia to collect trepang. The Bryant group then turned north to cross the Arafura Sea. Over the horizon was the island of Timor and their eventual freedom from the convict colony of Port Jackson. Their voyage up the east coast of Australia had been hazardous but successful due to William Bryant's judgement in choosing his fellow escapees and their ability to live off the land. They had been able to replenish their food and water supplies, and although their bodies were depleted, there had been no loss of life.

The cutter, with its nine convicts and two young children, landed at Kupang on 5 June 1791 after an epic voyage of 5200 km and 69 days. Their voyage from Port Jackson to Kupang in a small open boat has been compared to that of William Bligh and the castaways of the *Bounty*. William Bryant had the advantage of a route that included more coastal waters. However, it is generally agreed that each group performed an amazing feat, entitling them both to an important place in maritime history. As described by James Martin:

> We ran along the Island of Timor till we came to the Dutch settlement where we went on shore to the Governor House where he behaved extremely well to us filled our bellies and clothed double with everything that was wore on the island.

The convicts had prepared a story to explain their arrival at Kupang in a small boat. Bryant took his wife's maiden name, calling himself William Broad, and told the authorities that they were survivors of an English vessel shipwrecked on the Great Barrier Reef. The Dutch governor Timotheus Wanjon believed their story and provided them with accommodation, food and clothing. Bryant signed bills that the governor could then send to the British government for reimbursement. After two months of living in relative freedom, their comfortable existence ended abruptly in a bizarre turn of events. The group had been through so much together and overcame so many obstacles, yet for reasons that James Martin is unable to explain fully, William Bryant informed the Dutch of their escape from Sydney Cove:

> We remained very happy at our work for two months till William Bryant had words with his wife, went and informed against himself, wife and children and all of us, we were immediately taken prisoners and were put into the Castle where we were strictly examined.

One month later, on 17 September 1791, Captain Edwards of *HMS Pandora* arrived in Kupang in his own open boat. After landing, the governor informed him that he had eight males, one woman, and two children in custody whom he suspected had escaped from the convict colony at Sydney Cove. He related how they had arrived very distressed in June 1791 in an open six-oared boat and told him they had been shipwrecked onboard a vessel off the coast of New Holland.

Captain Edwards, the surviving *Bounty* mutineers, and the Port Jackson escapees embarked on the 6th of October aboard the Dutch vessel *Rembang* for Batavia. As Edwards later wrote to the Secretary of the Admiralty:

> Before we sailed, Governor Wanjon delivered to me eight men, one woman and two children who came to Kupang in June last in a six-oared cutter.

The group arrived at Batavia on the 7th of November, where the Dutch East India Company decided to divide the ship's company and prisoners among four of their ships proceeding to Holland. However, the heat, humidity, malaria, dysentery and typhus in Batavia claimed the lives of two of the Port Jackson escapees, as William Bryant died in Batavia along with his young son Emanuel.

Captain Edwards, several warrant officers, the ten surviving *Bounty* mutineers, and the remaining escaped male convicts from Port Jackson embarked on the *Vreedenburg*. According to George Hamilton, it was a tedious passage, with more deaths of those infected in Batavia, including the convicts Samuel Bird and William Morton. The convict James Cox decided to jump overboard in the Sunda Straits and attempt to swim to freedom. Mary Bryant and her daughter Charlotte took passage in the *Hoornweg*.

Upon reaching Capetown on 18 March 1792, Captain Edwards found *HMS Gorgon* moored there on its way back from Port Jackson. Consequently, the six surviving escapees were placed on board. According to Watkin Tench, Mary Bryant was greatly but discreetly admired, and he wrote:

> It was my fate to fall in again with part of this little band of adventurers. In March 1792, when I arrived in the *Gorgon*, at the

Cape of Good Hope, six of these people, including the woman and one child, were put on board us to be carried to England. Four had died, and one had jumped overboard at Batavia.

I confess that I never looked at these people without pity and astonishment. They had miscarried in a heroic struggle for liberty after having combated every hardship and conquered every difficulty. The woman, and one of the men, had gone out to Port Jackson in the ship which had transported me thither. They had both been always distinguished for good behaviour. And I could not but reflect with admiration at the strange combination of circumstances which had again brought us together, to baffle human foresight and confound human speculation.

To the credit of Captains Edwards and Captain Parker, these ill-fated people were never treated as prisoners, but mustered with the crews of the vessels they were in.

Sixteen days after the *Gorgon* sailed from Capetown, Lieutenant Clark noted in his journal, 'Very hot. Below the lower gun deck at night, there is hardly any living for the heat'. Five of the children of the marines died, and then, a few days later, he made the following entry:

> Squally weather with a great deal of rain all this day. Last night the child belonging to Mary Bryant, the convict woman who went away in the fishing boat from Port Jackson last year, died about four o'clock. Committed the body to the deep.

Mary Bryant and the other Port Jackson escapees – William Allen, Samuel Broom, Nathaniel Lillie and James Martin, arrived back in England on 18 June 1792. The punishment for escaping from transportation was death. However, when the press publicised the story of the escapees, there was considerable public sympathy for them, considering the hazardous voyage they had made to regain their liberty. The prisoners declared that 'they would sooner suffer death than return to Botany Bay' and, as the London Chronicle's reporter put it, 'His Majesty, who is ever willing to extend his mercy, surely never had objects more worthy of it' than these escapees from New South Wales.

Influential lawyer and author James Boswell, moved by their heroic odyssey, decided to support Mary and her companions at his own expense and lobbied the Home Secretary to help them gain pardons. When brought before the court on 7 July, they were all ordered to 'remain on their former sentence, until they should be discharged by course of law'. The Crown Prosecutor did not press for the full legal penalty, stating:

> The Government would not treat them with harshness, but, at the same time, would not do a kind thing to them, as they might give encouragement to others to escape.

Six weeks after her former sentence expired, on 2 May 1793, Mary Bryant was released from Newgate Prison with a free pardon. While William Allen, Samuel Broom, Nathaniel Lillie, and James Martin had to wait until 2 November 1793 before being released by proclamation. It is believed it was during this period of his detention that James Martin, together with the memories of his fellow convicts, wrote up his description of their escape from Port Jackson. This document was discovered in 1930 in the archive of one of Britain's great philosophers, Jeremy Bentham, who was one of the earliest and most implacable enemies of transportation to New South Wales and who had campaigned for the release of Mary Bryant and the other escapees after their return to England. The document is an important part of Australia's early history and the only first-hand account of the most famous escape from the penal colony at Sydney Cove by transported convicts.

10

William Bligh's Second Chance, 1791

> Perhaps no space of 3½ degrees in length presents more dangers than Torres Strait, but with caution and perseverance, Captains Bligh and Portlock proved them to be surmountable and within a reasonable time. How far it may be advisable to follow their track through the Strait, will appear more fully hereafter.
>
> Lieutenant Mathew Flinders, 1792

William Bligh was widely celebrated when his account of the mutiny was made public. In accordance with Naval Law, he had to face a court-martial for the loss of His Majesty's Armed Vessel *Bounty*. The other survivors of the mutiny and epic voyage were called to give testimony, and Bligh was 'most-honourably acquitted'. As a result, Bligh was presented to King George III, who directed that he go to Tahiti for a second time and carry out his previous instructions to collect the breadfruit plants and deliver them to the West Indies. A direction that could have been regarded as either a reward or punishment.

For this voyage, Bligh was given two ships. The *HMS Providence*, a new West Indiaman of four hundred tons, with a crew of one hundred men, including officers and marines, fitted out to accommodate six hundred breadfruit plants in the after-cabin. Also, *HMS Assistant*, a brig of one hundred tons commanded by Lieutenant Nathanial Portlock with a crew of twenty-five men. On board the *Providence* was a seventeen-year-old midshipman named Mathew Flinders, who was about to embark on the voyage of a lifetime. The vessels departed England on 3 August 1791, and it was significant that the voyage would include a detachment of twenty Marines.

Upon arrival in Tahiti, Captain Bligh met many of his old friends among the natives, who received him with every mark of joy. The chiefs related the story of the mutineers' return to Tahiti and their final departure. Bligh also learned of Captain Edwards's visit to the island and the capture of fourteen mutineers. Lieutenant George Tobin on the *Providence* describes their arrival in Tahiti:

> Before the vessels were scarcely at anchor, canoes laden with hogs and various fruits were about us in vast numbers, the natives bartering these articles for iron and other wares, Hatchets were in the greatest demand. Several chiefs came on board, and in the afternoon we were honoured with a visit from Itia, the queen, from whom it was understood that Pomare, the king was at Moorea, an island in sight to the westward. All the visitors expressed unfeigned joy and satisfaction at meeting their old friend Captain Bligh and agreeably to the custom of the island brought a present of cloth, hogs and fruit, the former being wrapped around him by Her Majesty. The beauty of her countenance and the elegance of her figure had felt the ravages of time, but there was in her deportment a complacency and good humour sensibly interesting.
>
> As the sun declined, the canoes returned onshore leaving by far the most desirable of their freight among our crew, which

after the trying self-denial of a long voyage, shut off from the dearest solace life affords, could not but be truly acceptable.

The *Providence* stayed for over three months in Matavai Bay, collecting 600 breadfruit plants and storing them aboard. After leaving, Bligh touched at the Cook Islands, Tonga and then the Fiji Islands in search of the remaining mutineers.

As before, the intent was to keep the breadfruit seedlings in a tropical climate for as long as possible, so the vessels were to sail through the Torres Strait and onwards to the Cape of Good Hope. It is not certain Captain Bligh would have chosen himself to relive the nightmare of his open boat voyage, but the Admiralty had instructed him to chart a safe passage through the sunken reefs and clusters of rocks of the Torres Strait.

The Great Barrier Reef is diminished to the north, where the fresh water and sediment flowing out of the Fly River of New Guinea inhibits coral growth. Bligh discovered an entrance into the Torres Strait between what he named Anchor Cay and Bramble Cay at the northernmost extent of the Reef. Now known as the Bligh Entrance, this is the best approach to the Great Northeast Channel and is now used regularly by commercial ships wanting to enter the Torres Strait from outside the Great Barrier Reef. Bligh would have had painful memories of his first voyage through the Torres Strait, but this voyage was much further to the north.

The ships edged forward for the next nineteen days, with the cutter sounding in the lead, followed by the *Assistant* and then the *Providence*. Anchoring at night and sending out boats at dawn to search for a safe passage to the west. It was slow, arduous work, with Bligh often conning the ship himself from the masthead. The result was the first survey done in the Straits, and a chart was drawn by Nathaniel Portlock, who commented:

> From the masthead, with a good lookout, you may see and avoid danger from the colour of the water. The bottom can be

seen in six or seven fathoms of water, many more I am confident. But people must not depend too much on this, for from six or seven fathoms you can step onto the reef which is not above two feet.

Torres Strait, the General Order of Sailing
George Tobin, State Library NSW

As you would expect, Bligh's log of his second voyage through the Torres Strait is full of dates, times, latitude and longitude, water depths, currents, tides, wind conditions and other important nautical information. However, it is the logs of his junior officers Mathew Flinders and George Tobin that are the most interesting, for they provide the first detailed descriptions of the Islanders and their watercraft. A professional artist who was meant to go on the voyage became ill, and George Tobin, the third Lieutenant on the *Providence*, became the ship's artist and has provided us with valuable visual documentation of the voyage

The cutter and the whaleboat, sounding ahead, led the *Assistant*, followed by the *Providence* into the Torres Strait. They followed the Great

Northeast Channel to the southwest until Erub Island was in view, which Bligh named Darnley Island after his distant relative, the Earl of Darnley. At daylight, a boat was sent to sound a passage near the island and we have this description from Mathew Flinders:

> Several large sailing canoes were seen, and the cutter making the signal for assistance, the pinnace was sent to her, well manned and armed.
>
> On the return of the boats in the afternoon, it appeared, that, of four canoes that used their efforts to get up to the cutter, one succeeded. There were in it fifteen Indians, black, and quite naked; and they made signs which were interpreted to be amicable. These signs the officer imitated; but not thinking it prudent to go so near as to take a green coconut, which was held up to him, he continued rowing for the ship. A man, who was sitting upon the shed erected in the centre of the canoe, then said something to those below; and immediately they began to string their bows. Two of them had already fitted arrows, when the officer judged it necessary to fire in his own defence. Six muskets were discharged; and the Indians fell flat into the bottom of the canoe, all except the man on the shed: the seventh musket was fired at him, and he fell also. During this time, the canoe dropped astern; and the three others having joined her, they all gave chase to the cutter, trying to cut her off from the ship; in which they would probably have succeeded, had not the pinnace arrived at that juncture, to her assistance. The Indians then hoisted their sails and steered for Darnley's Island.

Mathew Flinders had watched this encounter from the deck of the *Providence*, as he was obviously concerned for the safety of his fellow seamen. But his admiration of the skill of the natives in handling their canoes is notable since the Torres Strait Islanders had developed manoeuvrable craft, propelled by sails, sweeps or paddles, which could navigate these waters in each direction according to the tide and the wind, for he wrote:

> No boats could have been manoeuvred better, in working to windward, than were these long canoes by the naked savages. Had the four been able to reach the cutter, it is difficult to say, whether the superiority of our arms would have been equal to the great difference of numbers; considering the ferocity of these people, and the skill with which they seemed to manage their weapons.

The following day several canoes from Darnley Island came off towards both vessels. On approaching, the Islanders clapped upon their heads and exclaimed "Whou! Whou! Whoo!" repeatedly, with much vehemence; at the same time, they held out arrows and other weapons in exchange for "*toore-tooree*" by which they meant iron. It is Mathew Flinders who gives us this detailed description of the Islanders:

> After much difficulty, they were persuaded to come alongside and two men ventured into the ship. They had bushy hair -- were rather stout made -- and nearly answered the description given of the natives of New Guinea. The cartilage, between the nostrils, was cut away in both these people; and the lobes of their ears slit, and stretched to a great length, as had before been observed in a native of the Fiji Islands. They had no kind of clothing; but wore necklaces of cowrie shells, fastened to a braid of fibres; and some of their companions had pearl-oyster shells hung around their necks. In speaking to each other, their words seemed to be distinctly pronounced.
> Their arms were bows, arrows, and clubs, which they bartered for every kind of iron work with eagerness; but appeared to set little value on anything else. The bows are made of split bamboo, and so strong, that no man in the ship could bend one of them. The string is a broad slip of cane, fixed to one end of

the bow; and fitted with a noose, to go over the other end, when strung. The arrow is a cane of about four feet long, into which a pointed piece of the hard, heavy, casuarina wood, is firmly and neatly fitted; and some of them were barbed. Their clubs are made of casuarina and are powerful weapons.

As descendants of the Melanesians, the eastern Torres Strait Islanders were intimately familiar with the sea and sailing. Their watercraft were necessary for inter-island trade, and this exchange knotted islanders together in the reciprocal exchange of the goods necessary for life. Produce such as yams, sweet potatoes, bananas, taro and sugar cane was exchanged for turtles, dugong, coconuts, garden vegetables and timber for canoes. George Tobin gives a good description of the vessels used by the Islanders:

> Their canoes are up to 20 metres in length and appear to have been hollowed out of a single tree, but the pieces which form the gunwales are planks sewed on with the fibres of the coconut and secured with pegs. These vessels are low, forward, but rise abaft; and being narrow, are fitted with an outrigger on each side, to keep them steady. A raft, of greater breadth than the canoe, extends over about half the length; and upon this is fixed a shed or hut, thatched with palm leaves. These people, in short, appeared to be dextrous sailors and formidable warriors; and to be as much at ease in the water, as in their canoes. ... The sails of their canoes are made of matting in an oblong form rudely stitched together. The mast to which it is hoisted consists of two bamboo poles, the lower ends fixed close together in the bottom of the canoe and the upper ends extended the width of the sail, from whence it is hoisted travelling upon two guys. Some canoes have two sails. They are always fixed close together in the forepart of the canoe. We observe them always to row well to the windward before they set their sail, and I think they have a piece of plank which they sometimes use as a lee-board.

On September 8, *Providence* and *Assistant* reached a low islet towards the centre of the Torres Strait, which Bligh named Dalrymple Island after the British geographer Alexander Dalrymple, who, in 1769, whilst translating some Spanish documents, found a copy of Luís Vaz de Torres' long-forgotten letter to the King of Spain. Significantly, Dalrymple named the Torres Strait in honour of Luis Vaz de Torres.

After the *Providence* reached the central part of the Strait, it was confronted by reefs and shoals at every turn. Near Zagai Island, they were involved in a skirmish with natives in a flotilla of sailing canoes, which resulted in the death of several Islanders as well as the death of one crewman and the wounding of two others. We have a description of this encounter from Mathew Flinders:

> September 10. The boats sounded the channel to the northwest and finding sufficient water, the vessels got underway at noon to follow them. There were many natives collected upon the shore of Dungeness Island (Zagai Island) and several canoes from Warriors Island (Tudu Island) were about the brig. Presently, Captain Portlock (of the *Assistant*) made the signal for assistance, and there was a discharge of musketry and some guns, from his vessel and from the boats. Canoes were also coming towards the *Providence*, and when a musket was fired at the headmost, the natives set up a great shout, and paddled forward in a body, nor was musketry sufficient to make them desist. The second great gun, loaded with round and grape, was directed at the foremost of eight canoes, full of men; and the round shot, after raking the whole length, struck the high stem. The Indians lept out and swam towards their companions plunging constantly to avoid the musket balls which showered thickly about them. The squadron then made off, as fast as the people could paddle without showing themselves; but afterwards rallied at a greater distance until a shot which passed over their heads made them disperse and give up any idea of any further attack.

No arrows fell on board the *Providence*; but three men were wounded in the *Assistant*, and one of them afterwards died. The depth to which the arrows penetrated the decks and sides of the brig, was found to be truly astonishing.

Captain Bligh was clearly upset regarding this event, writing in his log, 'This was the most melancholy account I have received. All my hopes to have friendly intercourse with the natives were now lost'. The encounter occurred near Tudu Island, so Bligh named it Warrior Island, and the extensive reefs stretching away to the northeast, almost to the coast of Papua, were named Warrior Reefs.

The Providence and the Assistant required to fire at the canoes
George Tobin, State Library NSW

A southeast gale prevented the *Providence* and *Assistant* from proceeding for three days. In the meantime, the boats sounded the passage between the reefs to the northwest and found it to be about 5 fathoms. They were also sent to examine the passage around the southern reefs, which was found to be deeper. As described by Bligh, this was chosen as the preferable route.

> September 16. At half past 3 the *Assistant* got underway, and at half past 5 anchored near us. Lieutenant Portlock reported that he had not been able to weather the reef but had seen the eastern part from whence it had trended to the south-west. A large space was open to the S, West which made me determine to weigh with both vessels and explore that way. We were under sail at sunrise; nothing could exceed the regularity of the soundings. Everywhere the view was arrested by rocks, banks, and islands. The nearest land being S. 24 E, one mile and a half, was the north-westernmost of three of three islands. To the west and south of Jervis Island (Mabuig Island) lay an island we called Mulgrave Island (Badu Island). Further to the south was Banks' Island (Moa Island) with a very high round hill.

In this situation, the vessels were so closely surrounded by rocks and reefs that they had almost no swinging room. The wind blew a fresh gale, and a tide ran between four and five knots an hour. Therefore, it was impracticable to continue westward amid this labyrinth of dangers. An anxious night passed without incident, and we have this description from Flinders:

> Sept 18. The route was continued through the passage, between reefs and rocks, which, in some places, were not three quarters of a mile asunder; the smallest depth was 4 fathoms. On clearing this dangerous pass, which Captain Bligh named Bligh's Farewell (now known as the Bligh Channel) the ships anchored in 6 fathoms, sandy bottom, the wind blowing strong at S.E with thick weather.

The following day, the wind moderated, and the water depth gradually increased from 6 to 8 fathoms. To the west, there was now no land in sight. A new passage through the Torres Strait had been found and charted. Mathew Flinders wrote in his journal:

> Thus, was accomplished, in nineteen days, the passage from the Pacific, or Great Ocean, to the Indian Sea; without other misfortune than what arose from the attack of the natives and some damage done to the cables and anchors. Perhaps no space of 3½ degrees in length, presents more dangers than Torres' Strait; but, with caution and perseverance, the Captains Bligh and Portlock proved them to be surmountable and within a reasonable time. How far it may be advisable to follow their track through the Strait, will appear more fully hereafter.

Having cleared the Torres Strait, the *Providence* and the *Assistant* sailed across the Arafura Sea to their next destination, Kupang in Timor and the site of William Bligh's destination after crossing the Pacific in the *Bounty's* longboat. Bligh wrote in his log:

> October 2nd. At 1 o'clock we were nearly through the Straits of Samow when the southeast wind left us ... As soon as my people were a little refreshed I sent Lieutenant Guthrie to acquaint the Governor of my arrival. I also desired a pilot if any person was sufficiently acquainted with the roads. At 10 at night Mr.Guthrie returned. He had met a friendly reaction from Mr. Wanjon who was now the Governor and was told I should have every assistance. The captain of the *Verwagting* came to show us the way into the Road. He was called Tytrand Jacobus Bouberg and, having known me before, was kindly solicitous to give us assistance. With light winds in the morning to the northward in a couple of hours we got into Kupang Roads when the Fort saluted us with 15 guns, and the same on my landing.

Captain Bligh was welcomed by many old friends and found that Timotheus Wanjon, the gentleman who had assisted him so kindly when here in the *Bounty's* launch, was the new Governor. Important news awaited Bligh in Kupang: Captain Edwards had lost the *Pandora* while trying to enter the Torres Strait through a passage in the Great Barrier Reef. He had arrived at Kupang in four boats with the eighty-nine crew who had survived the wreck. Thirty-one of his crewmen had been lost at sea, including four of the Bounty prisoners. Bligh would have felt disappointed at the loss of some of the Bounty mutineers as his fervent wish was for them all to be returned to England for an Admiralty court-martial and sentence.

Transplanting the Breadfruit
Thomas Gosse, 1796, National Library of Australia

From Kupang, the ships sailed to the Cape of Good Hope and reached Port Royal, Jamaica, on February 4, 1793, where Bligh's task was successfully completed. He had redeemed himself, and presumably, King George was happy. The plants were in excellent condition, and the sugar planters voted Bligh a grant of 500 British pounds for his services. George Tobin wrote:

> Ten years have elapsed since this humane undertaking was suggested to our gracious sovereign by the West India planters through the medium, if I mistake not, of Sir Joseph Banks. Many unlooked for obstructions have intruded to prevent its earlier accomplishment. These, however, did not damp the zeal of its promotors ... that the introduction of this nutritious food into the sugar colonies will be attended with the most beneficial effects to the toiling Africans can hardly be doubted. Most of the edible plants in the West Indies are known to suffer and frequently to be wholly destroyed by the violence of hurricanes. This, we have reason to believe, will not be the case with the firm and prolific breadfruit tree, but that in the course of a few years, it will become the chief sustenance of a large proportion of our fellow creatures, whose lot in life loudly calls on our sympathy and consideration.

On 7 August 1793, the *Providence* moored at Deptford, two years and five days from the date of her departure. A few weeks later, Bligh delivered his logs, journals, and charts to the Admiralty. It can be said that Cook trained Bligh as a navigator and Bligh trained Flinders. However, it appears there were certain unwritten rules regarding who could name a chart. Bligh had drawn a manuscript chart of the passage through Torres Strait, showing the tracks of the *Endeavour*, the *Bounty*'s launch and the *Providence*. Flinders also drew a Torres Strait chart, entitled *A Chart of the Passage between New Holland and New Guinea as seen in His Majesty's Ship Providence in 1792* and intended to accompany his personal log. This is Flinders' first-known nautical chart, which he signed, M. Flinders. It had been prepared under Bligh's supervision, and the fact that he signed his own name may have been the cause of a dispute between the two men, as before the expedition returned to England, Bligh reduced Mathew Flinders to the rank of able seaman.

On their return in September 1793, Mathew Flinders' father wrote in his diary:

> By the mercy of Divine Providence of God – my son hath safe returned from his long and perilous voyage, completing it in little more than two years ... his Captain latterly was not on the best of terms with him, which was an unpleasant circumstance.

On returning to England, Bligh expected his accomplishment to earn him even greater acclaim. However, while he was away, the mutineers captured by Captain Edwards had been put on trial, and the emotional testimony of some of the defendants, along with the efforts of some influential families, including the family of Fletcher Christian, had swayed popular opinion against him. Peter Heywood, who had sided with the mutineers but did not play a major part in the crime, presented a lengthy defence of his actions that cast Bligh in a less favourable light. Though the public debate raged inconclusively, Bligh's reputation had been irreparably damaged and speculation about what could have driven so many respectable men to commit so disgraceful a crime became widespread.

It would be twenty years before the fate of the remaining *Bounty* mutineers was revealed. The American sealing ship *Topaz* was to visit Pitcairn Island, and its crew were the first to brave the surf, which crashed against its steep cliffs. The following message was received at the Admiralty in 1808:

> Captain Folger, of the American ship *Topaz*, of Boston, relates that, upon landing on Pitcairn's Island, in lat. 25° 2' S., long. 130° W., he found there an Englishman of the name of Alexander Smith, the only person remaining of nine that escaped in his Majesty's late ship *Bounty*. Smith relates that, after putting Captain Bligh in the boat, Christian, the leader of the mutiny, took command of the ship and went to Otaheite, where

the great part of the crew left her, except Christian, Smith, and seven others, whom each took wives and six Otaheitan menservants, and shortly after arrived at Pitcairn, where they ran the ship on shore, and broke her up; this event took place in the year 1790.

About four years after their arrival (a great jealousy existing), the Otaheitans secretly revolted and killed every Englishman except himself whom they severely wounded in the neck with a pistol ball. The same night, the widows of the deceased Englishmen arose and put to death the whole of the Otaheitans, leaving Smith, the only man alive on the island, with eight or nine women and several small children. During his recovery, he applied himself to tilling the ground so that it now produces plenty of yams, cocoanuts, bananas, plantains, hogs, and poultry. There are now some grown-up men and women, children of the mutineers, on the island, the whole population amounting to about thirty-five, who acknowledge Smith as father and commander of them all; they all speak English and have been educated by him (as Captain Folger represents) in a religious and moral way.

The second mate of the *Topaz* asserts that Christian, the ringleader, became insane shortly after their arrival on the island and threw himself off the rocks into the sea; another died of a fever before the massacre of the remaining six took place. The island is badly supplied with water, sufficient only for the present inhabitants, and no anchorage.

Extracted from the logbook of the *Topaz*, 29th Sept. 1808.
(Signed) 'WM. FITZMAURICE, Lieut. Valparaiso, Oct. 10th, 1808

11

Shah Hormuzeer and Headhunters in the Torres Strait, 1793

> In each of the huts, and usually on the right-hand side going in, were suspended two or three human skulls; and several strings of hands, five or six on a string. These were hung round a wooden image, rudely carved into the representation of a man, or of some bird.
>
> Journal of Captain William Bampton, 1793

By 1784, the English East India Company had become a colonial government and left its trade to private English merchants known as Country Traders, many of whom were former Company employees. One of the first private commercial voyages to New South Wales was by Captain William Brampton in the brig *Shah Hormuzeer* in 1793, when he sailed from India across southern Australia to bring cattle and rice to Port Jackson.

The prevailing winds aided a ship enroute to Australia to travel via the south coast and then return via the north coast of New Guinea to Batavia and then India. Governor Grose then chartered the *Shah Hormuzeer* and the South Sea whaler *Chesterfield* to take goods from Port Jackson to Norfolk Island, then sail to India and return with further supplies for the colony. It seems Captain Brampton knew little of how Cook or Bligh navigated the Torres Strait, but the motivation to take commercial advantage of this shortcut was strong. In June 1793, these two vessels sailed from Norfolk Island intending to pass through Torres Strait.

Natives and a canoe on Darnley Island
H.S. Melville, National Library of Australia

After sailing through the Bligh Entrance, they sighted an island in daylight on July 1 they named Tates Island (Darnley Island) (Erub). The ships anchored in 22 fathoms, and the boats were sent towards this island to see if it was inhabited. When the boats returned from Erub, they were followed by four canoes, one of which came alongside, and we have this description from Captain Brampton:

> Most of the natives had their ears perforated. Their hair was generally cut short; but some few had it flowing loose. It is naturally black; but from being rubbed with something, it had a reddish, or burnt appearance. The natives, so far as they could be understood, represented their island to abound in refreshments; and it was, therefore, determined to send another boat to make further examination.

On July 3, Mr Shaw, chief mate of the *Chesterfield*, Ascott, an ex-convict from Norfolk Island, Captain Hill of the New-South-Wales Corps and a passenger named Carter sailed in the whaleboat towards Darnley island with four Lascar seamen. They were expected to return the following day, but the 4th, 5th and 6th passed without their return. Inexplicably, the vessels waited three days before sending out a search party. On July 7th, two boats, manned and armed, under the command of Mr Dell, chief mate of the *Shah Hormuzeer*, were sent in search of the whaleboat.

On reaching the island, Mr Dell heard conch shells sounding from different directions and saw eighty or ninety armed natives upon the shore. From their inquiries, by signs, after the missing boat, the islanders indicated it had gone westward. As the boats searched the island, the natives followed along the shore in increasing numbers. One man, who appeared to be a chief, had a small axe in his hand, known from its red handle to belong to Mr Shaw. On reaching the bay on the north-west side of the island, Mr Dell noted that the natives disappeared, except about thirty, who were very anxious in persuading him to land. They brought down women and made signs that the boat and people whom he sought were a little way up on the island. However, when they rowed forward, they could see other natives who appeared to be lying in ambush.

On July 10, Captain Brampton landed an armed party of forty-four men on the island. They examined the native huts and found gruesome evidence of the fate of their missing shipmates – coats with buttons cut off, a tinder box, a lantern, and other articles from the whaleboat and, most disturbingly, three severed hands, one with distinctive marks which they thought belonged to Carter. There seemed no doubt of them having been murdered by the Islanders. This was shocking, especially the three severed hands. They presumed that not only had their companions been murdered, but their bodies had been mutilated, and perhaps worse.

In retribution, the armed party burnt and destroyed one-hundred-and-thirty-five huts, sixteen canoes measuring from fifty to seventy feet in length, and various plantations of sugar cane. The natives appeared to have retreated to the hills as none of them could be discovered. Despite these ravages committed by the armed party, somebody came up with a detailed description of the island:

> Darnley's Island was judged to be about fifteen miles in circumference. It is variegated with hills and plains, and the richness of the vegetation bespoke it to be very fertile; it appeared, however, to be scantily supplied with fresh water, there being only one small place where it was found near the shore. The plantations of the natives, which were extensive and numerous in the plains, contained yams, sweet potatoes, plantains, and sugar canes, enclosed within neat fences of bamboo; and cocoa-nut trees were very abundant, particularly near the habitations. The hills, which mostly occupy the middle of the island, were covered with trees and bushes of luxuriant growth; and upon different parts of the shores, the mangrove was produced in great plenty.
>
> The habitations of the Indians were generally placed at the heads of the small coves; and formed into villages of ten or twelve huts each, enclosed within a bamboo fence of, at least, twelve feet high. The hut much resembles a haycock, with a pole driven through it; and may contain a family of six or eight

people. The covering is of long grass, and cocoa leaves. The entrance is small; and so low, that the inhabitants must creep in and out; but the inside was clean and neat; and the pole that supports the roof, was painted red, apparently with ochre.

In each of the huts, and usually on the right-hand side going in, were suspended two or three human skulls; and several strings of hands, five or six on a string. These were hung round a wooden image, rudely carved into the representation of a man, or of some bird; and painted and decorated in a curious manner: the feathers of the Emu or Cassowary generally formed one of the ornaments. In one hut, containing a much greater number of skulls, a kind of gum was found burning before one of these images.

On July 11, the *Shah Hormuzeer* and the *Chesterfield* steered northward, with soundings of 15 to 19 fathoms. After running three hours with a fresh breeze, a reef and sand bank were seen ahead, and the ship veered to the southwest. Both ships anchored at what they named Chesterfield Island (Ugar). An armed party was immediately sent ashore to obtain intelligence about the lost whaleboat and crew. The natives were assembled in hostile array upon the hills, sounding their conch shells, but they fled after launching a few arrows. Several islanders were wounded by the shots fired in return, but they succeeded in escaping to a canoe at the rear of the island.

In the afternoon of July 13, the ships proceeded westward, but after meeting with many reefs, they sailed north and reached Bristow Island (Bobo Island), lying close to the coast of New Guinea. Attempts to find a passage here were fruitless, and after the *Chesterfield* ran aground, they returned to their former anchorage at Chesterfield Island (Ugar) on July 21. Two native canoes immediately came off the island, and one of the islanders remained on board the *Shah Hormuzeer* until eight o'clock that evening. He seemed to be without fear, and when an inquiry was made about the lost boat and people, he pointed to a whaleboat and made signs that one had been at Darnley's Island, and that six of the people were killed. This was valuable information, and many presents were made to this man.

On July 26, the ships slowly proceeded to the south and turned westward. On the morning of the 27th, they were at anchor in 11 fathoms near what they called Colvins Island (Dungeness Island). With the ship's boats, they explored Dove Island to the south, and we have this description of the island:

> Dove Island is about one mile and a half in circumference; and covered with trees and shrubs, the fragrance of whose flowers perfumed the air. Amongst other birds, two beautiful doves were shot. The plumage of the body was green; the head, bill, and legs, red; the tail, and undersides of the wings, yellow. No huts, plantations, or other signs of fixed inhabitants were seen; nor was there any fresh water.

On August 1, they proceeded westward towards what they called Reeves Island when the *Chesterfield* struck upon a bank, but the coral gave way to the ship, and she went over without damage. In the evening, they anchored in 4½ fathoms at Duncan's Island (Turn-again Island) (Buru), and Captain Bampton noted in his log:

> The more we proceed westward, the more intricate our passage appears, we are now completely entangled between the reefs and shoals and I believe we should find it as difficult to find our way back as we should in proceeding forward.

The *Shah Hormuzeer* and the *Chesterfield* remained here for seventeen days because of the strong southeast winds that blew most of the time. They were now running out of food and fresh water. Small quantities of fish, crabs, and shellfish could be found on the island. But the well they dug produced little water; however, Captain Bampton ingeniously contrived a still. He had a cover, with a hole in the centre, fitted upon a large cooking pot and over the hole, he placed an inverted tea kettle with the spout cut off. To the stump of the spout was fitted a part of the tube of a speaking trumpet, and this was lengthened by a gun barrel, which passed through a cask of salt water, serving as a cooler. From this contraption, good fresh water was produced to twenty-five to forty gallons per day.

At daylight on August 22, they followed the long boat to the northwest. At seven o'clock, the *Shah Hormuzeer* grounded in 2 fathoms upon a bank near Talbot's Island (Boigu Island near the New Guinea coast). She remained upon this bank until the morning of the 24th when the vessel was floated off. It did not appear to have received any damage other than the loss of the false keel. On August 29, the *Shah Hormuzeer* grounded again. When the ship floated, they made sail westward, and the water deepened to 9 and 12 fathoms. At noon, it had again shoaled to 6 fathoms, and after proceeding a little further westward, they anchored near what they later named Deliverance Island.

On the 31st, after leaving the appropriately named Deliverance Island, the ships steered southwestward, leaving on the starboard a very extensive bank on which the long boat had sounded 2 fathoms. The latitude was 9° 27' at noon, and no land was in sight. The soundings then increased gradually; at sunset, no bottom could be found, and a swell coming from the open sea announced that the dangers of Torres Strait were surmounted.

In this attempt to pass through the Torres Strait by a northern route, they found themselves surrounded by reefs and sandbanks, so progress was slow. Captain Bampton's chart of the *Shah Hormuzeer's* track through the Strait shows the vessels zigzagging and doubling back upon themselves in trying to find a safe passage through its reefs. The passage through the Strait lasted seventy-two days. It was the longest voyage to date, but it was significant as it was the first crossing of the Torres Strait by a commercial vessel.

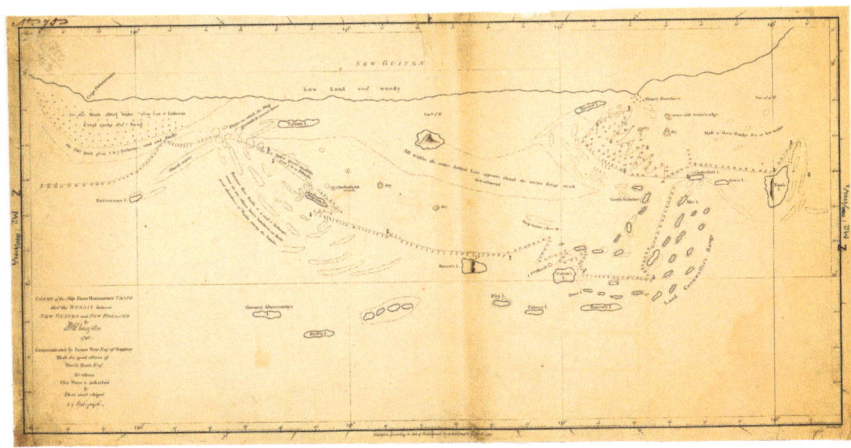

Captain Bampton's chart of the voyage, 1793

The voyage had cost the lives of the eight men who had gone ashore on Erub, they were all believed dead, but a year later, two survivors turned up on the Dutch island of Banda. According to their account, the whaleboat party was attacked as soon as they came ashore, but Shaw, Carter, and Ascott managed to get back in the boat and beat a hasty retreat. They were without provisions or a compass, and it was impossible to reach the other ships, so they bore away to the west, hoping to make Timor. After ten days of privation, they reached the island of Timor Laut (Tanimbar), where Carter subsequently died. After some time on the island, Shaw and Ascott sailed with a local prahu for the island of Banda, which they reached in April of the following year and reported to the Dutch colonial authorities. They eventually reached Batavia and then returned to England.

News of the murders at Darnley Island would have been passed on to the English East India Company, then to the Admiralty, and a warning given that the presence of native Head-hunters was a danger to any shipping passing through the Torres Strait.

12

Mathew Flinders sails to Port Jackson, 1795

> Mr Bass and myself hailed it with joy and mutual congratulation, as announcing the completion of our long-wished-for discovery of a passage into the Southern Indian Ocean.
>
> Mathew Flinders, 1798

In August 1793, when the *Providence* and the *Assistant* returned to England from their voyage to collect breadfruit plants, they found their home ports alive with wartime activity. A revolutionary France had become a potential threat to the Kingdom of England, and the Royal Navy was again preparing for war. In October, Mathew Flinders joined the *Bellerophon* as a midshipman and on June 1, 1794, he participated in the first naval battle of the war and the ensuing victory over the French Fleet in the Atlantic which was described as 'the glorious First of June'.

A New Chart of New Holland on which are delineated New South Wales and a plan of Botany Bay, 1787
Andrews

On 16 February 1795, Mathew Flinders sailed for Port Jackson as the Senior Masters Mate on *HMS Reliance*, bringing Captain John Hunter back to the distant colony to become the new Governor-General. Also on board was the ship's surgeon, George Bass. A man who was everything that Flinders wanted to be: physically imposing, intellectually adventurous, fluent in several languages, an accomplished surgeon, a scholar, and a man of action. Flinders was profoundly impressed with George Bass, and they became great friends. Years later, he wrote:

> In Mr. George Bass, surgeon of the *Reliance*, I had the happiness to find a man whose ardour for discovery was not repressed by any obstacles, nor deterred by danger; and with this friend a determination was formed of completing the examination of the east coast of New South Wales, by all such opportunities as the duty of the ship and procurable means, would allow.

Flinders knew that there had been no significant mapping of the coastlines of New Holland and New South Wales since Cook's charting of the east coast in 1770. The map shows the remaining uncharted sections of the continent, which are the southern coast from Ceduna to Point Hicks, the northern part of Van Diemen's Land and the northeast coast between Lizard Island and the Providential Channel, where the *Endeavour* was outside the Barrier Reef.

A month passed after Bass and Flinders stepped ashore in Port Jackson before they set off in a rowboat, appropriately named the *Tom Thumb*, to explore Botany Bay and the Georges River. Later, while Flinders was busy supervising repairs to the *Reliance*, George Bass sailed a ship's whaleboat further south with six naval seamen, entering the Bass Strait and reaching as far as Westernport Bay.

In forwarding Bass's chart to the Colonial Secretary, Governor Hunter wrote:

> From this little sketch it will appear ... that the high land in latitude 39 degrees south ... is the southern extremity of this country, and that the land called Van Diemens is a group of islands ... probably leaving a safe and navigable passage between; to ascertain this is of some importance. I am endeavouring to fit out a decked boat of about fifteen tons burden for that purpose, in which I propose to send two officers.

The two officers were George Bass and Mathew Flinders, who, in October 1798, departed Port Jackson in the sloop *Norfolk* with eight seamen and the aboriginal guide Bungaree. The *Norfolk* was small for an extended voyage, however, there was no argument from Flinders, whose promotion to lieutenant meant he was now officially qualified for command, and he wrote:

> Should a strait be found, it is intended to pass through it and return by the south end of Van Diemen's Land; making such examinations and surveys on the way as circumstances might permit. Twelve weeks were allowed for the performance of this service, and provisions for that time were put on board; the rest of the equipment was completed by Captain Waterhouse of the *Reliance*. I had the happiness to associate my friend Bass in this new expedition.

Mathew Flinders was now in command of his first independent voyage of exploration, an opportunity to gain practical experience in a voyage he considered extremely important and would shape his future naval career. Unfortunately, his efforts were hampered by the sloop's poor steering compass, the lack of an azimuth compass, and a chronometer to calculate longitude, an omission he remarked several times in his reports. Flinders now experienced the thrill of standing on the deck of his first command while charting a coastline that no European navigator had ever traversed. After passing what is now called Flinders Island in the eastern part of the Strait, they sailed west along the northern coast of Van Diemens Land. On reaching Cape Grim, on the north-west peninsula of Van Diemen's Land, they saw a great swell breaking on the rocks, and Flinders wrote:

> Mr Bass and myself hailed it with joy and mutual congratulation, as announcing the completion of our long-wished-for discovery of a passage into the Southern Indian Ocean.

Flinders had made a running survey from offshore, with little detail; some sections he left as blank spaces, and he recorded few place names. However, one peak about eight miles inland he called Mount Norfolk after his vessel, and on the west coast, he named Mount Heemskirk and Mount Zeehan after the two ships of the Tasman expedition that first discovered Van Diemen's Land in 1642. After circumnavigating the island, they returned to Port Jackson on January 11, 1799.

The discovery of Bass Strait was important because it shortened the route from the Cape of Good Hope to Port Jackson by 900 kilometres, roughly a week's sailing and avoided many of the wild storms of the southern ocean. Mathew Flinders had proved his skill as an explorer, dealing with all hazards, charting the coastline and, thanks to the assistance of Bungaree, meeting on friendly terms with the Aborigines. The evidence of his skill lay in the map of Van Diemen's Land he produced, even though he considered it imperfect 'because no timekeeper could be procured' to calculate longitude accurately.

Map of Van Diemen's Land, 1798-99
Mathew Flinders, National Maritime Museum UK

In March 1800, Flinders departed Port Jackson on the *Reliance* and, sailing across the Pacific and around Cape Horn, arrived back in England after an absence of five and a half years. He then arranged the publication of his 42-page memoir, *Observations on the Coast of Van Diemen's Land, Bass's Strait and its islands, and Part of the Coasts of New South Wales; intended to accompany the Charts of the late discoveries in those Countries. By Mathew Flinders, Second Lieutenant of His Majesty's Ship Reliance*, complete with a dedication to Joseph Banks with the usual adulatory praise.

Joseph Banks had been personally responsible for founding the convict colony at Port Jackson and was at the height of his power and influence. Interested in putting the colony on a better financial footing, he had written to the Under-Secretary John King in May 1798:

> We have now possessed the country of New South Wales more than ten years, and so much has the discovery of the interior been neglected that no one article has hitherto been discovered by the importation of which the mother country can receive any degree of return for the cost of founding and hitherto maintaining the colony.
>
> It is impossible to conceive that such a body of land, as large as all Europe, does not produce vast rivers, capable of being navigated, that such a country, situated in a most fruitful climate, should not produce some native raw material of importance to a manufacturing country as England.

A copy of Banks' letter had reached Governor Hunter at Port Jackson that same year, and he likely passed the knowledge of this proposal on to Flinders. Since Cook's survey of the east coast in 1770, very little more had been learned about the continent's shores. Flinders would have realised that this was an opportunity for himself in an area where he knew he was better qualified than almost anyone else. Just eleven days after his return to England, Flinders wrote to Joseph Banks and put forward a plan for the circumnavigation of Australia. This seems impetuous, but he had the whole voyage home to contemplate his plan. Flinders had now turned twenty-five, and despite the achievements of having proven the existence of Bass's Strait and having circumnavigated Van Diemen's Land, there had been neither reward nor recognition other than the recommendations of his immediate superiors. He openly revealed his personal ambitions in his letter to Joseph Banks:

> I have too much ambition to rest in the unnoticed middle order of mankind. Since neither birth nor fortune have favoured me, my actions shall speak to the world. In the regular service of the Navy there are too many competitors for fame. I have

therefore chosen a branch which, although less rewarding by rank and fortune, is yet little less in celebrity.

Flinders proposed a full scientific expedition to survey the entire coast of New Holland for possible harbours and rivers that could provide access to the interior. While an on-board party of scientists and artists would explore the land's natural resources. This was to be a scientific expedition in the style of Cook, although with a more openly colonial and commercial purpose. He began his letter by referring to his charts of Bass's Strait and Van Diemen's Land and then stating his desire to carry out the work that Banks himself had proposed:

> It cannot be doubted, but that a very great part of that still extensive country remains either totally unknown or has been partially examined at a time when navigation was much less advanced than at present. If his Majesty should be so far desirous to have the discovery of New Holland completed ... and the late discoveries in that country should so far meet approbation as to induce the execution of it to be committed to me, I should enter upon it with that zeal which I hope has hitherto characterised my service.

After an anxious delay of two months, Flinders was invited to meet with Joseph Banks at his mansion in Soho Square. He had acquired a powerful patron, and only five days after their meeting, the Admiralty selected a ship for the voyage and ordered the Navy Board to begin her refit. Mathew Flinders had placed himself in 'the right place at the right time' because what had caused such a rapid response was a request from the French for a passport guaranteeing safe passage for a scientific voyage to New Holland and New South Wales under the command of Nicolas Baudin. The Admiralty had little choice but to grant them a passport. But they were aware of the potential embarrassment of France exploring, naming and even colonising what they considered a British possession. Flinders could not believe his good luck and wrote to his fiancé Ann Chapelle:

> A ship is fitting out for me to go out to New South Wales. She is to be ready, it is said, in the beginning of January. An astronomer and a naturalist are already engaged, and draftsmen are searching for. Everything seems to bespeak the utmost haste, but my appointment is not yet given out ... It seems, that promotion cannot accompany any appointment to the command of her; there are however, some promises made on that head, to take place shortly.

The ship selected for this voyage of exploration was a collier of three-hundred and thirty-four tons, which the Royal Navy had bought, converted into a sloop-of-war and renamed *HMS Investigator*. Flinders received his commission as commander on 16 February while he was busy at Sheerness Harbour preparing for the voyage. The newest and best supplies were ordered for the vessel, and topmasts, spare sails, and naval stores were loaded. Most importantly, all the surveying and navigational instruments necessary for charting New Holland's coasts were ordered, including four box chronometers, two of which were made by Thomas Earnshaw.

During all this preparation, Flinders applied for a week's leave to visit his family. There, he made a sudden and impetuous decision. He would marry Ann Chapelle and sail together to New South Wales on the *Investigator*. The marriage occurred on 17 April 1801 in the Lincolnshire village of Partney, and they returned to board the *Investigator*. Naval wives rarely travelled in His Majesty's Ships and certainly not without permission. Flinders believed she could travel with or without permission, and Ann sailed with him on the *Investigator* from Sheerness Harbour in the Thames Estuary to Portsmouth, the port of departure. Naval gossip reached the Admiralty and Sir Joseph Banks that Mrs Flinders was now living on the ship, and she intended to sail to New South Wales. On 21 May, this letter came from his patron:

> Dear Sir,
>
> I have but just time to tell you that news of your marriage, which was published in the Lincoln papers has reached me. The Lords of the Admiralty have heard also that Mrs Flinders is on the *HMS Investigator*, and that you have some thoughts of carrying her to sea with you. This I am very sorry to hear, and if that is the case I beg to give you my advice, by no means to venture to measures so contrary to the regulations and the discipline of the Navy; for I am convinced, by the language I have heard, that their Lordships will, if they hear of her being in New South Wales, immediately order you to be super-ceded.

Mathew Flinders had to choose between his love and career, and we all know the answer. The command of this voyage of exploration was to be the pinnacle of his career and deliver his hopes for fame and wealth. He would surrender his wife for the voyage! Poor Ann had said farewell to her family and friends because she would sail with her husband to Port Jackson. She would now have to return home after only a few months of wedded bliss, without her husband and perhaps without any future. She must have been completely devastated; worse, they did not meet again for another nine years. Flinders wrote to Joseph Banks saying:

> Whatever may be my disappointment, I shall give up the wife for the voyage of discovery, and I would beg of you, Sir Joseph, to be assured that even this circumstance will not damp the ardour I feel to accomplish the important purpose of the present voyage; and in a way that I shall preclude the necessity of anyone following after me to explore.

The *Investigator* took on the remaining crew and supplies while at Portsmouth waiting for final orders. Flinders was also waiting for his French Passport, which would protect him and his expedition from hostile interference if France and England were again at war. On 17 July, a packet arrived from the Admiralty, including his French passport, and on 20 July 1801, the *Investigator* sailed from Spithead.

Sailing via the Cape of Good Hope, Flinders landed at King Georges Sound, near modern-day Albany, and explored the area for a month. He knew from the Tasman Map of 1644 that Francois Thijssen had charted the south coast of New Holland in the *Gulden Zeepaard* as far as Ceduna. For nine days and 435 nautical miles, Flinders followed the steep cliffs that rise three hundred metres above the Southern Ocean, which he named The Great Australian Bight, until he reached the islands of Saint Francis and Saint Peter, as named by Thijssen, and which Flinders named the Nuyts Archipelago to honour the Dutch explorers.

Flinders had been instructed to search for a strait that might link the southern coast to the Gulf of Carpentaria and separate the continent. On the morning of February 21, 1802, the *Investigator* reached what appeared to be a large Gulf, and he could view the coast bearing northeast until it was lost from sight. Was this the Gulf they were looking for? And he described the animated discussions held on board the ship that night:

> Deep inlets, inland seas and passages into the Gulf of Carpentaria, were terms frequently used in our conversations of this evening, and the prospect of making an interesting discovery, seemed to have infused new life and vigour into every man on the ship.

After sailing north for more than a week, the water ended, and he named it Spencer Gulf after the First Lord of the Admiralty. While Flinders continued charting the southern coast, they encountered another ship on 8 April 1802 in the large open bay, which Flinders later named Encounter Bay. It was the French ship *Geographe*, commanded by Captain Nicolas Baudin. Flinders with Robert Brown, acting as translator, rowed across to the French ship and after the customary exchange of courtesies, Flinders asked for Baudin's passport from the Admiralty, which he inspected and then offered his in exchange, which Baudin handed back without looking at it. This meeting was a surprise for both Captains but more so for the French. The British were uncomfortably aware of the French expedition's sailing, but Baudin did not know of the Flinders voyage, which had left months after his own departure from Le Havre.

Although Flinders had been commissioned to search for large rivers capable of navigating into the interior of the continent, both he and Baudin failed to observe that the lakes on the eastern shoreline of Encounter Bay were an entrance into the Murray River, which is the only river on the whole continent which could provide significant access into the interior. The *Investigator* subsequently completed charting the southern coast through Bass Strait before arriving in Port Jackson on 8 May 1802. The Colony had a new Governor, Phillip Gidley King, and Flinders would have been impressed by the improvements in Sydney since he was last there in 1795.

There would be no letters from his wife Ann for another year, but Mathew Flinders wrote a long letter to her from Port Jackson, lamenting their sad parting, describing his voyage out, and encouraging her to be cheerful:

> Let not unavailing sorrow increase thy malady, but look my dear Ann to the happy side. See me engaged, successfully thus far, in the cause of science and followed by good wishes and approbation of the world ... hastening to thy love as the best reward for all my toils.

Mathew Flinders, Port Jackson, 1802

13

Mathew Flinders circumnavigates New Holland, 1803

> No person must expect to know reefs as they would islands or can passages be easily followed amongst them: the strictest and most constant attention is requisite to it. A different time of tide makes a great difference in the appearance of reefs.
>
> Mathew Flinders, 1802

Mathew Flinders had now completed surveying some of the gaps in the map of New Holland and New South Wales from 1778, including both the mapping of Van Diemens Land and the south coast of the mainland from Ceduna to Point Hicks. His next mission would be to sail north and fill in the gap in Cook's 1770 map when he was outside the Great Barrier Reef.

Flinders needed to supplement his crew after losing eight men, presumed drowned, at the entrance to Spencer Gulf. The only men available were convicts, and of the nine men selected, all except two were under a life sentence. However, Phillip Gidley King granted that on the completion of the voyage, they could receive conditional emancipation or absolute pardons based on the recommendations of Mathew Flinders, who wrote:

> Finding it impossible to fill the compliment with free people, I applied to the Governor for his permission to enter such convicts as should present themselves ... when the requisite number were selected, he gave me an official document, containing clauses relative to these men, well calculated to ensure their good conduct.

On the morning of 22 July 1802, the *Investigator* with the brig *Lady Nelson* made sail in a fresh breeze from Port Jackson, passed between the Sydney Heads, and turned north into the Pacific Ocean. The Admiralty's directions for the voyage instructed Flinders to conduct a careful investigation and accurate survey of the Torres Strait, as finding a safe and timely passage through the Strait would benefit the English East India Company's commercial trade. Flinders wrote:

> The Navigation from the Pacific, or Great Ocean, to all parts of India, and to the Cape of Good Hope, would be greatly facilitated if a passage through the Strait, moderately free from danger, could be discovered; since five or six weeks off the usual route, by the north of New Guinea or the more eastern islands, would thereby be saved.

Flinders obtained Governor King's permission to take on Bungaree as an aboriginal guide as he had helped calm several dangerous skirmishes during the *Norfolk* voyage around Van Diemens Land, and Flinders wrote:

> I had before experienced much advantage from the presence of a native from Port Jackson, in bringing about a friendly

intercourse with the inhabitants of other parts of the coast ... Bungaree, the worthy and brave fellow who had sailed with me in the *Norfolk*, now volunteered again; the other was Nanbaree, a good natured lad.

That his famous black cat, Trim, was besotted with Bungaree further cemented Flinder's affection, 'If he had occasion to drink, he mewed to Bungaree and leapt up onto the water cask; if to eat, he called him down below and went straight to his kit, where there was generally a remnant of a black swan. In short, Bungaree was his great resource, and his kindness was repaid with caresses'.

Unfortunately, Flinders ignored instructions from the Admiralty to proceed directly to the Torres Strait, affecting the results of the rest of his voyage. Cook's running survey of the East Coast had been undertaken without a chronometer, and Flinders could now calculate longitude with far greater accuracy. New sophisticated theodolites also enabled angular distances to be measured along both vertical and horizontal planes. Flinders thus saw himself as one of a new breed of professional navigators who could turn the art of surveying into a science. His ambition was to survey the coastline so comprehensively that it would never need doing again and to prove that he could exceed the great James Cook:

> Those who reflect ... and consider that Captain Cook was liable to all the errors of first examination and was without a timekeeper, will readily understand why I have ventured to take such great liberties with the works of so greatly and justly distinguished a navigator; and these circumstances shall be my apology. If the corrections shall be found to approximate the truth I shall be excused; if it should prove otherwise I shall never excuse myself.

Flinders should have sailed directly north to chart the gap that appeared on Cook's chart of the east coast between Lizard Island and

Providential Channel when the *Endeavour* was outside the Barrier Reef. However, he wasted valuable time charting parts of the coast that Cook had already mapped and now had to hurry north to the Torres Strait before the onset of the northwest monsoon. He then lost more time searching for a way through the outer coral barrier. Channels between the reefs turned into torrents with the rush of incoming and outgoing tides, resulting in a succession of snapped anchor cables. Eventually, he abandoned the endless little winding waterways and steered north in the smooth water inside the larger reefs, looking for a sufficiently wide opening to the sea. *Lady Nelson* regularly lagged behind and had difficulty beating to the windward, and then she lost her false keel after being grounded. The vessel had become more of a hindrance than a help, and Flinders decided she would have to return to Port Jackson.

> October 10. My anxious desire to get out to sea, and reach the north coast before the unfavourable monsoons should set in, had led me to persevere amongst these intricate passages beyond what prudence could approve; for had the wind come to blow too strong, and no anchors, in such deep water and upon loose sand could have held the ship; a rocky bottom cut the cables; and to have been under sail in the night was certain destruction. I therefore formed the determination, in our future search for a passage out, to avoid all narrow channels, and run along, within sight the larger reefs, until a good safe opening should present itself.

Somewhere near the Whitsunday Islands, Flinders decided to wait until low water when many reefs would dry and the channels between them would become more visible, and he marvelled at the shapes of the corals:

> We had wheat sheaves, mushrooms, stag horns, cabbage leaves, and a variety of other forms, glowing underwater with vivid tints of every shade betwixt green, purple, brown, and

white; equalling in beauty and excelling in grandeur the most favourite parterre of the curious florist ... but whilst contemplating the richness of the scene, we could not long forget with what destruction it was pregnant.

It is important to note that Mathew Flinders was the first person to recognise that the Barrier Reef stretches for 2300 kilometres in a single connected line from Hervey Bay in Queensland to near the coast of New Guinea. It was Flinders who named it the Great Barrier Reef, and he wrote:

> I therefore assume it as a great probability that with the exception of this and perhaps several small openings, our Barrier Reefs are connected with the Labyrinth of Captain Cook; and that they reach to the Torres Strait and to New Guinea through 14 degrees of latitude: which is not to be equalled in any other known part of the world.

Flinders eventually found a gap through the Great Barrier Reef and into the Coral Sea. He continued sailing north until he found himself outside the Torres Strait, where he could sight Murray Island. However, the heavy banks of monsoonal cloud gathering overhead suggested there would be no time to carry out his orders for a careful and accurate survey of the Torres Strait:

> 27 OCTOBER 1802. The wind, which had been at southeast, then shifted suddenly to north, and blew fresh with squally weather; but at midnight it veered to south-east again. These changes were accompanied by thunder, lightning and rain; indications, as I feared, of the approaching northwest monsoon.
>
> 28 OCTOBER 1802. Our latitude at noon was exactly that of the opening that Captain Edwards of the *Pandora* had encountered in 1791 and which I call Pandora's Entrance. This opening appeared to be preferable to that further northward, by which

Captain Bligh and Mr. Bampton had got within the reefs, more especially as it led directly for Murray's Islands (Mer), where, if possible, I intended to anchor.

The heavy banks of cloud accumulating overhead suggested there would be no time to carry out the orders for a careful and accurate survey of the Torres Strait. The ships' boats would now act as survey vessels ahead of the *Investigator* as they edged their way through the myriad reefs and shoals of the Torres Strait. It would have been much safer to sail further north and find the Bligh Entrance, through which Flinders had already sailed on the *Providence,* but he wanted to find a more direct route into the Strait from where Murray Island could be sighted. Cook and the *Endeavour* had taken only three days to traverse the Strait from the inner reef. Bligh with the *Providence* had spent nineteen days traversing the Strait from the outer reef. The tortuous passage of the *Shah Hormuzeer* and *Chesterfield* through the northern strait had lasted as long as seventy-two days. Flinders hoped to find a much quicker and easier route from outside the Great Barrier Reef:

> 29 OCTOBER 1802. Finding by the latitude that we had been set considerable to the north, and were out of the parallel of Murray's Islands, I tacked to the SSW; and at two o'clock, the largest island was seen bearing S38W about 5 leagues. Soon afterward, a reef came in sight to the south-east, extending in patches towards the islands; and presently another was distinguished to the westwards, from the masthead, which took nearly a parallel direction, the passage between them being about four miles wide.

Fortuitously, Flinders discovered what is now called the Flinders Entrance into the Torres Strait, which provides a direct southwest route to the Murray Islands (Mer). The *Investigator* anchored under the lee of the largest of these islands on 29 October, and we have Flinders's description of the island:

> Murray's largest island is nearly two miles long, by something more than one in breadth; it is rather high land, and the hill at its western end may be seen from a ship's deck at the distance of eight or nine leagues, in a clear day ... On the shores of the large island were many huts, surrounded by palisades, apparently of bamboo; cocoa-nut trees were abundant, both on the low grounds and the sides of the hills, and plantains, with some other fruits, had been brought to us.

The canoes of the Torres Strait Islanders are what makes them unique compared to the Australian aborigines. Mathew Flinders had been impressed by their sailing skills on his first voyage through the Torres Strait, and we have this description as they sailed towards the *Investigator*:

> The two masts, when not wanted, are laid along the gunwales; when set up, they stand abreast of each other in the fore part of the canoe and seemed to be secured by one set of shrouds, with a stay from one masthead to the other. The sail is extended between them; but when going with a side wind, the lee mast is brought aft by a backstay, and the sail then stands obliquely. In other words, they brace up by setting in the head of the lee mast, and perhaps the foot also; and can then lie within seven points of the wind, and possibly nearer. This was their mode, so far as a distant view would admit of judging; but how these long canoes keep to the wind, and make such way as they do, without any after sail, I am at a loss to know.

Flinders did not forget that the inhabitants of these islands had made an attack upon the *Providence* and *Assistant* in 1792, and he probably knew of the killing of men from the merchant ship *Chesterfield* at Erub in 1793. For this reason, the marines were kept under arms, the guns clear, matches lit, and officers stationed to watch each canoe that came near the ship. The *Investigator* had scarcely anchored when between forty and fifty Islanders came out in three canoes. They would not come alongside the ship but lay off at a little distance, holding up cocoa nuts, joints of bamboo filled with water, plantains, bows and arrows, and yelling *tooree! tooree!* (iron, iron). A barter soon commenced and was carried on in this manner:

> A hatchet, or other piece of iron being held up, they offered a bunch of green plantains, a bow and quiver of arrows, or what they judged would be received in exchange; signs of acceptance being made, the Indian leaped overboard with his barter, and handed it to a man who went down the side to him; and receiving his hatchet, swam back to the canoe. Some delivered their articles without any distrust of the exchange, but this was not always the case. Their eagerness to get *tooree* was great, and at first, anything of that same metal was received but afterwards, if a nail were held up to an Indian, he shook his head, striking the edge of his right hand upon the left arm, in the attitude of chopping; and he was well enough understood.

View of Murray's Isles with the natives offering to barter.
William Westall 1802. National Library of Australia

Some of the Islanders were allowed to come on board the *Investigator* bringing bows and arrows, pearl shells and necklaces of cowrie shells to trade, which allowed Flinders to observe them at close quarters and give us this description:

> The colour of these Indians is a dark chocolate; they are active, muscular men, about the middle size, and their countenances expressive of a quick apprehension. Their features and hair appeared to be similar to those of the natives of New South Wales, and they also go quite naked; but some of them had ornaments of shell work, and of plaited hair or fibres of bark, about their waists, necks, and ankles. Our friend Bungaree could not understand anything of their language, nor did they pay much attention to him; he seemed, indeed, to feel his own inferiority, and made but a poor figure amongst them.

The *Investigator* sailed on, and in the late afternoon, they reached what Flinders named Half-Way Island, which is scarcely more than a mile in circumference and was one of the sand cays produced by the washing up of broken coral. Some banks have become islands; some are above the high-water mark but have no vegetation, while others overflow at every high tide. Flinders had to navigate his way between these islands or half-islands and the reefs below the water line, and he wrote:

> No person must expect to know reefs as they would islands or can passages be easily followed amongst them: the strictest and most constant attention is requisite to it. A different time of tide makes a great difference in the appearance of reefs.

The next day, heavy winds swept through the Strait. The *Investigator* found shelter on the lee of a large island, which Flinders identified as Wednesday Island, as named by Bligh on his open boat voyage to Timor. Flinders had a copy of Bligh's chart made during this desperate voyage and was most impressed that the chart provided more precise drawings of certain sections of the coastline than Cook's version. He was full of praise for William Bligh and wrote:

> To the west of Cape Cornwall, the islands ... have less agreement both in situation and appearance with Captain Cook's chart, than they have with that made by Captain Bligh in the Bounty's launch. It has been a cause of much surprise, that under such distress of hunger and fatigue and of anxiety still greater than these, and whilst running before a strong breeze in an open boat, Captain Bligh should have been able to gather materials for a chart; but that this chart should possess a considerable share of accuracy, is a subject for admiration.

From Wednesday Island, Flinders found and charted the modern Prince of Wales Passage through the Torres Strait, which is still favoured by most commercial shipping. Conscious of his Admiralty orders to focus on a close survey of the Torres Strait, he wrote explaining that the impending monsoon had prevented this. However, he still felt pleased as he had accomplished his passage through the Torres Strait from outside the Great Barrier Reef in only six days when the usual voyage around the north coast of New Guinea would take six weeks. The *Investigator* now turned south to sail down the west coast of Cape York and follow the voyages of the Dutch explorers.

> 6 NOVEMBER 1802 The *HMS Investigator* passed Batavia River (Pennefather River) at the distance of six miles, with soundings of 5 to 8 fathoms. The botanical gentlemen being desirous of seeing the productions of this part of the country, the whaleboat was lowered down, and they went to examine the inlet ... There was a good deal of difficulty getting in on account of the shoals. On the north side was a party of natives, and Bungaree went on shore to them, naked and unarmed, but although provided with spears, they retreated from him, and all our endeavours to bring about an interview were unsuccessful.

> 10 NOVEMBER 1802 We passed the southern extremity of Cape Keer-Weer (Cape Turnabout). This point is one of the very few remarkable projections to be found on this low coast, but it is not noticed on the Dutch chart; there is little doubt however, it was seen in 1606, in the yacht *Duyfken*, the first vessel which discovered any part of Carpentaria; and so that the remembrance may not be lost, I gave the name of the vessel to the point - Duyfken Point.

The ship's carpenter had reported to Flinders that while traversing the Torres Strait, the *Investigator* had been leaking at the rate of 10-14 inches per hour. The outright peril this suggested was horrifying. However, nothing could be done until they found a suitable place to careen the vessel and inspect her hull. When they reached the southern part of the Gulf of Carpentaria, a suitable place was found to careen the ship between Bentinck and Sweers Island, a channel called Investigator Road. Many of the ship's timbers were found to be rotten, and planks, bends, timbers and tree nails on both port and starboard sides were affected. The prognosis was stark: if caught in a strong gale, the *Investigator* would founder; if grounded on a shoal, she would probably fall apart.

Considering the ship's condition, they needed to return to Port Jackson as soon as reasonably possible. Since the westerly monsoonal winds were now blowing, it would have been possible to return eastward through the Torres Strait. Possible, but dangerously possible, since the *Investigator* could easily be grounded on a reef or shoal. Flinders considered the dangers of an eastwards traverse of the Torres Strait in stormy weather and decided to continue in a westerly direction:

> From the above dreadful state of the ship, I find the complete examination of this country, which is one of the nearest objects to my heart, to be greatly impeded if not destroyed. I have hitherto considered that my business is to make so accurate an examination of New Holland that there should be no necessity

for any further navigator to come after me ... with the blessing of God, I would not have left anything of import to be discovered hereafter upon any of the shore of this great country.

The debilitated state of my health, as well as of many others on the ship, and a lameness in both feet from incorrigible scorbutic ulcers, render me unable to go about any longer in the boats, or to the masthead of the ship, both of which are absolutely necessary to any tolerable accuracy in this kind of surveying. I suppose it is unnecessary to state that the whole of this important part of our duty rests upon me: for Port Jackson, then, we now steered away with a fresh and fair wind.

Before they could return to Port Jackson, they desperately needed to resupply, as the sailor's health was disintegrating as fast as the ship's planks. Flinders had known the effects of scurvy on the health of the Baudin expedition before he left Sydney, but presumably, the supplies available from the Sydney colony were limited, and they were unwilling, unable, or ignorant of the curative effects of fresh vegetables to collect many of these from the Murray Islanders. This necessitated a trip to Timor and Kupang as the winter season was fast advancing on the south coast of Australia, and the poor state of the ship might have caused more labour at the pumps than the crew could exert. When the *Investigator* arrived in Kupang, the ship's surgeon reported that 22 men were suffering from scurvy:

31 MARCH 1803. Our supplies for the ship, procured at Kupang, were rice, arrack, sugar and the palm syrup called gulah; with fresh meat, fruit and vegetables during our stay, and for ten days afterwards ... tea, sugar candy, and some other articles for our messes, were purchased at the little shops kept by the Chinese-Malays; and poultry was obtained alongside by barter.

These fresh supplies helped prevent scurvy, but unfortunately, some of the ship's crew fell ill from drinking polluted water in Kupang, which, because of their weakened condition, led to death. From Timor, the *HMS Investigator* steered well clear of the west coast of New Holland on a course for Cape Leeuwin and then along the south coast. Flinders wished to do more charting in Bass's Strait, but because of the declining health of his crew, he could not stop:

> 23 MAY 1803. It was a great mortification to be thus obliged to pass Hunter's Isles and the north coast of Van Diemen's Land, without correcting their positions in longitude from the errors which the want of a timekeeper in the *Norfolk* had made unavoidable ... but when I contemplated eighteen of my men below, several of whom were stretched in their hammocks almost without hope and reflected that the lives of the rest depended upon our speedy arrival in port, every other consideration vanished; and I carried all possible sail, day and night, making such observations only as could be done without causing delay.

Mathew Flinders completed the first circumnavigation of New Holland and charted hundreds of miles of the coast when the *Investigator* sailed into Port Jackson on June 9, 1803, His voyages of 1802-3 confirmed that the continent was a single land mass, and the information needed to compile the first complete map of New Holland and New South Wales had been collected. It was, however, at the expense of the lives of one-quarter of his crew, as nineteen of them had died of either scurvy or dysentery during the voyage, and it also had affected Flinders's own personal health.

14

Mathew Flinders's third voyage through the Torres Strait, 1803.

> A captain who wishes to make the experiment of getting through the Barrier Reef must not be one who throws his ship's head round in a hurry so soon as breakers are announced from aloft. If he does not feel his nerves strong enough to thread the needle, as it is called, amongst the reefs, while he directs the steerage from the masthead, I would strongly recommend him not to approach this part of the coast.
>
> Mathew Flinders

After the *Investigator* reached Port Jackson in an unseaworthy state in July 1803, the Governor of New South Wales, Philip Gidley King, arranged for Mathew Flinders to sail back to England through the Torres Strait in the colonial ship *Porpoise*, together with the merchant ships *Cato* and *Bridgewater*. King also instructed that the voyage should allow Flinders time to explore the route through the Torres Strait in more detail.

Wreck of the Porpoise and Cato 200 miles from Land
Thomas Tegg, 1808

Returning to England would never be easy for Flinders, as the *Porpoise* and the *Cato* struck an unmarked reef in the Coral Sea, one thousand kilometres northeast of Port Jackson, which was to become known as Wreck Reef. The *Porpoise* had gone aground broadside to the reef with her hull facing the crashing waves, offering some protection to those onboard. The *Cato* was not so lucky. She had run aground with her deck exposed to the full force of the powerful waves and soon started breaking up with its crew desperately clinging to the wreckage:

> In a short time the decks and holds were torn up, and everything washed away; and the sole place left, where the unfortunate people could hope to avoid the fury of the sea ... they

all crowded together ... some lashing themselves to the timber heads, others clinging to the chain plates, and dead eyes, and to each other.

The survivors managed to reach a small sand cay named Wreck Reef Bank. Over the next several days, they salvaged as much as they could from the two stranded vessels. Casks of water, flour, salt meat, rice and spirits, and live sheep and pigs were all brought ashore, sufficient provisions to last the 94 castaways for three months. Fortunately, Flinders was able to save his manuscript and charts. As the survivors waited anxiously on the tiny cay, and only just above sea level, Flinders and thirteen others sailed for Port Jackson in the ship's cutter to bring help to the castaways.

Returning from Port Jackson, Flinders commanded the colonial schooner *Cumberland* to rescue the remaining survivors. They were transferred to the East Indiaman *Rolla* to take them back to Britain via Canton, while the *Cumberland* would proceed through the Torres Strait and directly across the Indian Ocean to the Cape of Good Hope. Flinders described the *Cumberland* as very leaky as water washed onto his cabin floor. He wrote that 'she sailed exceedingly crank and that writing his chronicle was like writing on horseback on a rainy day'. Worse than that were his fellow passengers:

> Of all the filthy little things I ever saw, this schooner, for bugs, lice, fleas, weevils, mosquitos, cockroaches and mice, rises superior to them all. We have almost got the better of the fleas, lice and mosquitos, but in spite of boiling water and daily destruction amongst them, the bugs still keep their ground ... I shall set my old friend Trim to work upon the mice.

On his third voyage through the Torres Strait, Flinders followed a channel through the Great Barrier Reef, which became known as the Cumberland Passage, that was some five miles to the south of the *Investigator*'s former track:

> This opening is a mile wide, and lies five or six miles, nearly E. N. E., from the largest of Murray's Islands; it would consequently be more direct to pass through it than to follow the *Investigator's* track around the north-eastern reefs; but from the narrowness of the opening and the many green spots where the depth is unknown to me, I dare not recommend it to a large ship, although it is very practicable for small vessels in fine weather.

Flinders knew that the Murray Islands were not always visible, and not every ship's captain could accurately calculate his latitude, especially in poor weather. It takes a brave captain and a cool head to breach the gaps in the Great Barrier Reef, and he wrote:

> A captain who wishes to make the experiment of getting through the Barrier Reef must not be one who throws his ship's head round in a hurry so soon as breakers are announced from aloft. If he does not feel his nerves strong enough to thread the needle, as it is called, amongst the reefs, while he directs the steerage from the masthead, I would strongly recommend him not to approach this part of the coast.

The familiar difficulties of traversing Torres Strait were constantly in Flinders' mind, which demanded his constant alertness as commander of the vessel. His route in the *Cumberland* then lay to the north of Wednesday Island before following the Prince of Wales Channel and sailing directly westward towards Booby Island and completing the traverse in 3 days. Flinders then made for Kupang to resupply and repair the *Cumberland*, which was found to be very leaky even while at anchor in the harbour. This was November, and Flinders was anxious to depart before the arrival of the north-west monsoon:

> I should have risked staying two or three days longer, had Kupang furnished the means of fresh boring and fitting the pumps, or if pitch could have been procured to pay the seams in the upper works after they were caulked; but no assistance in this way could be obtained; we, however, got a leak stopped in the bow, and the vessel was afterwards tight so long as she remained at anchor.

The *Cumberland* continued leaking badly, and its two pumps barely kept ahead of the water. When one of the pumps broke down, Flinders made the fateful choice in December 1803 to put it into the island of Mauritius to make the necessary repairs. Unfortunately for him, France was again at war with Britain, and the French Governor of Mauritius suspected him of being a spy. Flinders believed he would have the protection of his French passport; however, his passport referred to the *Investigator* and not the *Cumberland*, and for various reasons, he found himself detained for the next six years. Unfortunately, Trim disappeared during their stay in Mauritius, and a heartbroken Flinders no longer had him for company. Flinders dreamed of returning to England to live with his wife Ann and his faithful cat Trim in a country cottage, and he wrote:

> If ever I have the happiness to enjoy repose in my native country, there will be a place for Trim: under a thatched cottage surrounded by half an acre of land ... in a retired corner, a monument to perpetuate thy memory and record thy uncommon merits.

Had Flinders swallowed his pride and recognised that some deference was due to the official head of the colony of a foreign nation with whom his country was at war, his troubles might have been averted. In referring to General DeCaen, he wrote in a letter to Ann:

> I am not without friends even among the French. On the contrary. I have several, and but one enemy, unfortunately the last, is all-powerful here ... Did the governor know from what he keeps me, and what ecstatic happiness awaits my return, the least spark of humanity would be sufficient to make him hasten instead of retard my departure, but the man has no humanity for Englishmen.

While in Mauritius, Flinders began work on his general chart of Terra Australis. After more than a year in detention, he sent some documents, including his chart, to the Admiralty as John Aken, the Master of the *Cumberland*, was granted permission to leave Mauritius on an American ship in 1805:

> I then resolved to make good use of the opportunity presented by Mr. Aken's departure, and from this time to that of his sailing, was fully occupied in making up my despatches; and Mr Aken's health being improved, he took up residence in the Garden Prison for the purpose of giving his assistance.
>
> Besides a general chart of Terra Australis, showing the whole of my discoveries, examinations and tracks in abridgment, this packet for the Admiralty contained nine sheets upon a scale of four inches to a degree of longitude, and three sheets of particular parts in a larger size; also five chapters of a memoir explanatory of their construction, of the changes in the variation on shipboard, etc.; an enlarged copy of my log book, with remarks and astronomical observations from the commencement of the voyage to quitting the north coast of Terra Australis in March 1803; and a book containing all the bearings and angles which entered into the construction of the charts. The timekeeper, with the mathematical and nautical instruments belonging to the Navy Board were also sent; and either the original or a copy of everything in my possession which related either to the *HMS Investigator* or the voyage.

John Aken left Mauritius on a ship bound for New York, taking with him all the charts that Flinders had finished up to that date, as well as the large general chart of Terra Australis showing the extent of the new discoveries and all papers relating to the *Investigator's* voyage. Aken eventually arrived in London and delivered the Flinders charts and a copy of his logbook to Joseph Banks. On 4 October 1805, Aken wrote to Banks:

> Capt. Flinders is very desirous to know what steps have been taken for his release so that he may be a better judge of how to act himself. I believe he explained to you in his letter what the papers and charts were that I brought home.
>
> I left that great navigator, the companion of my misfortunes, on the 20th of May last, in good health, and high spirits expecting his release to be sent from Europe - every day.
>
> If you wish to see me, I will call on you with much pleasure and elucidate anything you may inquire after respecting Capt. Flinders.

Mathew Flinders believed that one reason for his detention was to give time for the description of the Baudin voyage and the French map of New Holland to be published first, and he wrote:

> Some odd opinions were stated relative to the real cause of my confinement ... in matters of discovery, I should think that he kept me here to give time for Captain Baudin's voyage to be published before mine, as no probable reason has been given for my detention it may possibly be so.

Banks received Flinders charts from John Aken in 1805, including his general chart of Terra Australis. If Banks had forwarded these on to the Admiralty and they had taken the initiative to publish, then

Flinders's map of Australia would have preceded the French map, and his would have been the first complete map of Terra Australis.

Joseph Banks and many others tried to get Flinders released. Even letters signed by Napoleon Bonaparte were sent to free him from 'house arrest' on the island. However, Flinders was prevented from returning to England until September 1810. Eventually, Flinders received this letter from Colonel Monistrol authorising his return to England:

> His Excellency the captain-general charges me to have the honour of informing you, that he authorises you to return to your country in the *Harriet* on condition of not serving in a hostile manner against France or its allies during the course of the present war.

This portrait of a gaunt-looking Mathew Flinders was completed in Mauritius before his departure. Arriving back in London in October 1810, Flinders hastily arranged lodgings and called upon the Admiralty before, at long last, meeting with Ann.

Portrait of Mathew Flinders from Mauritius aged 32,
Toussaint Antoine de Chazel 1806

Mathew and Ann Flinders had only spent a brief three months together after their marriage before Mathew left for Australia and a prolonged absence of almost ten years. It must have been an extremely emotional and tearful reunion. John Franklin, a cousin and former crew member, witnessed the reunion. Himself overcome with emotion, Franklin wrote to Flinders afterwards explaining the abrupt manner of his departure:

> I felt so sensibly, the affecting scene of your meeting Mrs Flinders

that I would not have remained any longer in the room under any consideration.

Flinders may have been correct that his detention on Mauritius was to give the French time to publish their chart of Australia. For the French account by Péron and Freycinet of the Baudin Expedition, the *Voyage de découvertes aux Terres Australes*, was published in 1811, including the French map of New Holland, the *Carte Générale de la Nouvelle Hollande* by Louis Freycinet. The most significant feature of this map is the naming of the south coast between Ceduna and Wilson Promontory as *Terre Napoleon*.

After his return to England, Flinders spent over three years preparing an account and an atlas of his voyage in the *Investigator*, the first expedition to circumnavigate Australia. It took this long because Flinders was meticulous in preparing his manuscript and charts, but he was also seriously ill. What he described as gravel (crystals) in his bladder caused considerable pain, which interrupted his work on the proof sheets. Although he was only 39 years, Ann describes how he had taken on the appearance of a 70-year-old. The book was to be his last testament, *and* 'A Voyage to Terra Australis', consisting of two large volumes and an atlas, was published in 1814, with Flinders tragically dying as the first copies came off the press.

One of the plates in 'A Voyage to Terra Australis' comprised a map of Torres Strait, presenting the tracks followed by Cook, Bligh, Bampton and himself. Flinders knew that much more exploratory work was necessary for the navigation of the Torres Strait to be mastered, and he thought it was likely that an easier route could still be found. However, when the Admiralty's Hydrographic Office published a guide that included instructions for sailing through Torres Strait in 1859, the various options for a passage were carefully considered. The verdict was that the route through Endeavour Strait, charted by Cook, should not be followed because it had dangerous sunken banks on the west, the route followed by Bligh in the *Providence* should be avoided owing to rapid and uncertain tidal streams, but the route through the Flinders

Passage and the Prince of Wales Channel, as navigated by Mathew Flinders, offered the safest and most direct east-west passage through Torres Strait.

Flinders had demonstrated in his 1814 chart that the New Holland of the Dutch and the New South Wales of the British were part of a single continent. He is now best remembered because his map of the island continent in 'A Voyage to Terra Australis' was the first to use the name Australia as he labelled his map 'General Chart of Terra Australis or Australia'. It was Joseph Banks and John Arrowsmith who preferred the term Terra Australis, but Flinders wrote in a footnote:

> Had I permitted myself any innovation upon the original term, it would have been to convert it into Australia: as being more agreeable to the ear, and as an assimilation to the names of the other great portions of the earth.

General Chart of Terra Australis or Australia
Mathew Flinders, 1814, State Library NSW

Mathew Flinders was buried in the St. James burial ground. However, his headstone was removed from St James's during the later expansion of Euston Railway Station, and his remains were believed to be lost. To mark the centenary of his death, a sculpture was commissioned in 2014. He is depicted bent over a map of Australia, holding the instruments he used to survey the continent. His faithful cat, Trim, is by his side, adding a playful dimension to the composition. It was decided to put the sculpture outside Euston station, close to where he was thought to be buried. Remarkably, archaeologists working on England's High Speed 2 rail project at Euston Station in 2019 found several coffins under Platform 15 and could identify Flinders' remains by the lead plate on the top.

15

Phillip Parker King completes the mapping of Australia, 1818

> If the sun is too clouded at noon to measure latitude, then the navigator is placed in a very anxious and unenviable situation, for the currents are so strong, that if the position of the ship is not accurately known then there is a risk being carried onto the Barrier Reef.
>
> Phillip Parker King

Phillip Parker King was born in 1791 on Norfolk Island as the son of its then Governor, Phillip Gidley King and his wife, Anna Coombe, and he was sent to England for his education at the age of eight. In 1807, he joined the Royal Navy as a sixteen-year-old and later saw action against the French in the Bay of Biscay and elsewhere. However, after the English defeat of Napoleon at the Battle of Waterloo, the great run-down of the Royal Navy's ships began. In 1815, it had over 700 ships in commission; three years later, only 130 were left. Thousands of seamen were discharged, and four of five commissioned officers were ashore on half pay with little chance of getting a ship again.

Mathew Flinders had known the father, Phillip Gidley King when he was Governor of New South Wales and had become a family friend. In 1811, he introduced the young Phillip Parker King to Sir Joseph Banks at a social event at Bank's house in Soho Square, where Captain Thomas Hurd was also present. Captain Hurd's proposal to form a Naval Hydrographic Service had fallen on deaf ears, and he sought the assistance of Joseph Banks.

Flinders's 1814 map of Australia was incomplete because he had not surveyed the gap in the map by James Cook when he sailed outside the Great Barrier Reef. After the problems with the *Investigator* and the declining health of his crew, he had been unable to chart the west coast of Australia, the outline of which had remained virtually unchanged since the Tasman Map of 1644. Lord Bathurst, as the Secretary of State for War and Colonies, agreed that finishing the charting of Australia would grant a political benefit to the Crown and scientific laurels to England. Thus 1817, the Royal Navy Hydrographic Service was created, and further exploration of the Australian coast was approved.

Captain Hurd assigned Phillip Parker King to complete Mathew Flinders' charting of Australia. However, the Navy could provide no ships and only two men as crew. King and the midshipmen Roe and Bedwell would sail to Port Jackson on a merchant ship, and King would have to find a suitable vessel and crew when they arrived. He was instructed to report to both the Colonial Department and the Navy, whose instructions were suitably vague:

> The arrangements for providing you with a proper vessel and crew, and other necessaries for the prosecution of the service having been made by the Colonial Department, my Lords have no directions to give you on these subjects, but to recommend you in the conduct and discipline of the vessel which may be entrusted to your care, to confirm, as far as practical, to the established usages of the Navy, and to the regulations for

preserving health, cleanliness and good order, which have been employed in His Majesty's ships on voyages of discovery.

Unfortunately, there was no proper vessel in Port Jackson until the arrival of the English cutter *Mermaid* from India. She was small, of 84 tons burden, 56 feet in length, 18 feet in beam, and with a draught of 9 feet, but her construction seemed sound, and there was no other choice. King convinced Governor Macquarie to purchase the vessel, and on 16 October 1817, *HMC Mermaid* was commissioned into the Royal Navy with the white ensign flying at her stern. However, considerable repairs and additions were required before she could sail on an extended voyage of exploration. The botanist Allan Cunningham joined the vessel plus twelve convict seamen, two boys and the esteemable Bungaree as an aboriginal guide. King's first mission was to chart the north and north-west coast of Australia between the North-West Cape and Arnhem land, parts of which had not been surveyed since Abel Tasman in 1644 and William Dampier in 1699, and which was carried out by King and the *Mermaid* between February and July 1818.

After returning to Port Jackson from this voyage, the *Mermaid* was prepared for a voyage north towards the Great Barrier Reef and Cook's Labyrinth. The part of the Inner Reef between Cape Flattery and the Providential Channel, when the Endeavour was outside the Great Barrier Reef, had remained unexplored until in 1815, when Lieutenant Charles Jeffreys in the colonial Brig *Kangaroo* had sailed the entire inner route on his way to Ceylon. However, he did not describe the route in detail, and King wanted to conduct a proper naval survey. The Colonial Government needed to have this route adequately charted, for compared to the shipwrecks that had occurred while trying to find a passage through the Great Barrier Reef into the Torres Strait, a voyage along a properly charted inner passage should be much safer and of value for commercial trade.

On 8 May 1819, the *Mermaid* sailed from Sydney, and with a moderate south-westerly wind, she was quickly out to sea and heading north. Early in the afternoon of June 1, the masthead lookout saw the outline of Cape Capricorn. They were now sailing among the reef-fringed islands of the inner Barrier Reef, and here, King's work of charting a route north to Cape York and through the Torres Strait began. On June 27, the *Mermaid* arrived at the Endeavour River and moored at the same position where Cook had careened the *Endeavour*. They expected to be in the river for a week, and before landing their tents and equipment onshore, King fired the grass, for he knew of Cook's experience there when the aborigines fired the grass at their campsite.

The Mermaid anchored at Endeavour River,
Phillip Parker King, State Library of New South Wales

On 12 July, they sailed out of the river and began running north with a fresh southeast wind. Sailing during the day and under clear skies, they passed Lizard Island and Cook's Passage. From here, King mapped the section of the Inner Passage that was missing from Cook's map. In broad daylight, it was easy for the crew to estimate depths by the colour of the water: light brown indicated danger, light blue was deeper water, and dark blue indicated the deepest water. After passing Restoration Island, King now had Bligh's track chart to use as a guide. When they reached Turtle Head Island, the wind turned to gale force. They entered a river that might provide protected anchorage, but instead, they struck the bar, with each wave lifting the *Mermaid* and then flinging her down with a shuddering crash. This could have been the end, but fortunately, a large wave drove her forward off the sand bank. King believed they had been saved by the hand of God, and he wrote:

> Some hideous rocks just rearing their rugged heads above the water would have inevitably proved our instantaneous and total destruction had not kind Providence ordered otherwise and assisted us by judicious management of the sails in getting us off into deeper water.

To commemorate this, King named it Escape River. However, they had not really escaped, for that night, the storm continued to rage. Even though anchored in the lee of Turtle Head Island, a particularly violent blow parted their anchor ring, and the *Mermaid* began drifting downwind before the next anchor held. After these narrow escapes, they passed through the channel between Cape York and Mount Adolphus Island and into the Torres Strait. They sailed around the north side of Wednesday Island and found anchorage at the south end of Good's Island (Palilug). Here they lost another anchor when the strong currents caused it to drag, and one of its flukes was broken clean off.

According to Phillip Parker King, the advantages of sailing the Inner Passage to the Torres Strait were that the seas were smoother, wood and water were generally available, and grass could be cut for livestock if necessary. Vessels would need to find anchorage every night, which meant a good night's rest for the crew. King thought the two routes were 'equally quick', but sailing the outer passage included the risks of running onto an uncharted reef and when strong currents and cloudy skies prevailed, there were difficulties in determining their exact position, and he wrote that:

> If the sun is too clouded at noon to measure latitude, then

the navigator is placed in a very anxious and unenviable situation, for the currents are so strong, and if the position of the ship is not accurately known then there is a risk of being carried onto the Barrier Reef.

After clearing the Torres Strait on July 25, 1818, the *Mermaid* crossed the Gulf of Carpentaria to commence surveying eastern Arnhem Land and to join up with their previous survey from earlier that year. In September, they reached the Kimberly coast, and the *Mermaid* was taking on so much water that urgent repairs were made at what they called Careening Bay. This took two weeks, but the ship was literally falling apart, and the only option was to return to Sydney as soon as possible. To voyage home, they sailed far off the west coast of New Holland until they reached 42 degrees south, where they were blown east by the 'Roaring Forties' with large, cold, following swells and sailed 640 miles in five days to reach the Bass Strait. On the afternoon of 28 November, they passed Wilsons Promontory and turned northwards to Port Jackson.

The *Mermaid* had continued taking on water during the voyage, and as it had been necessary to man the pumps, the crew were increasingly exhausted. On December 3, they were only forty-five miles south of Port Jackson but in poor weather, with pouring rain and an increasing onshore gale. Here, the *Mermaid* almost failed to complete her voyage around Australia. Worn down by anxiety and responsibility, it seems that King had underestimated the westerly set of the gale, as suddenly flashes of lightning lit the stormy sea, revealing they were heading for the cliffs of Cape Banks at the northerly point of Botany Bay and King wrote:

> Our escape appeared only possible through the intervention of Divine Providence, for, by the glare of a vivid stream of forked lightning, the extremity of the reef was seen within ten yards from our lee bow; and the wave which floated the vessel the next moment broke upon the rocks with surf as high as the vessels masthead; at this dreadful moment the swell left the

cutter, and she struck upon a rock with such force that the rudder was nearly lifted out of the gudgeons; fortunately we had a brave man and a good seaman at the helm for instantly recovering the tiller, after he had been knocked down when the vessel struck, he obeyed my orders with such attention and alacrity that the sails were kept full and the next moment a flash of lightning showed to our almost unbelieving eyes that we had passed the extremity of the rocks and were in safety.

The Mermaid off Cape Banks
Conrad Martens c 1840, National Library of Australia.

The *Mermaid* sheltered in Botany Bay until the gale blew itself out. On 9 December 1818, six months after she had left to chart the northern coast of Australia, she entered Port Jackson. As a result of Phillip Parker King's voyages in the *Mermaid*, the 'General Chart of Terra Australis or Australia' published in 1814 by Mathew Flinders was republished as the 'General Chart of Terra Australis or Australia corrected to 1829', including the section of the Queensland coast left blank by James Cook and then Mathew Flinders. Significantly, the corrected map included the seal of the Naval Hydrographical Office, under the authority of Captain Hurd, Hydrographer to the Admiralty.

General Chart of Terra Australis or Australia corrected to 1829
State Library NSW

King was now recognised as one of Britain's leading hydrographers and, in February 1824, was made a fellow of the Royal Society. In London in 1826, he published his two-volume *'Narrative of a Survey of the Intertropical and Western Coasts of Australia, performed between 1818 and 1822 and partly illustrated by his own sketches'*. King was the first and, for years, the only Australian-born person to attain eminence outside the Australian colonies, and he was promoted to Rear Admiral on the retired list before he died in 1856.

16

West to East - The Voyage of the Zenobia, 1823

> A passage through Torres Strait in the opposite direction – from the Indian Sea to the Great Ocean - has not, to my knowledge, been attempted and I have some doubt of its practicability.
>
> Mathew Flinders

It was equally important for colonial trade that a west-to-east passage could be made through the Torres Strait on a voyage from the Asian ports to Port Jackson.

A navigable western entrance to the Torres Strait had eluded the Dutch explorers, including Willem Jansz, Jan Carstenz and Abel Tasman. Jansz had sailed north past Hoogh Eylandt (High Island, Prince of Wales Island, Muralag) and only saw a shallow embayment. Carstenz entered the Endeavour Strait from the west as far as what he named *Rivier van Speult* (Jardine River) and probably concluded that sailing through shallow waters against the prevailing winds and currents was impossible. Abel Tasman had been instructed to again search for a navigable western entrance to the Torres Strait, had he arrived at the Endeavour Strait a month earlier, when the westerly monsoon was still blowing, a west-to-east voyage may have been possible.

Mathew Flinders had charted a practical east-to-west crossing of the Torres Strait by sailing up the outside of the Great Barrier Reef, entering through the Flinders Passage and exiting through the Prince of Wales channel, in a crossing of the Torres Strait, which could be made in only three days. But a passage from west to east was another matter, and he wrote:

> A passage through Torres Strait in the opposite direction – from the Indian Sea to the Great Ocean - it has not, to my knowledge, been attempted and I have some doubt of its practicability. A ship would have an advantage in entering the strait by its least dangerous side; but as the passage could be made only in December, January, or February, the rainy squally weather which probably will then prevail, would augment the danger from the reefs tenfold. The experiment is therefore too hazardous for any except a ship of discovery; whose business it is to encounter, and even to seek danger, when it may produce any important benefit to geography and navigation.

There is a period from November to February when the winds reverse under the influence of the Westerly Monsoon, as it crosses the Indonesian Archipelago. However, these winds also bring storms and monsoonal rain to the Gulf of Carpentaria and the Torres Strait. Captain James Horsburgh was the author of the precisely titled *'Directions for Sailing to and from the East Indies, China, New Holland, Cape of Good Hope, and the interjacent Ports, compiled chiefly from original Journals and Observations made during 21 years' experience in navigating those Seas'*. Known as the *India Directory*, it was compiled from original journals and observations made by himself and other ship captains. Published in 1808, it was an important source of information on winds, weather, waves, seasons, currents, barometers, waterspouts, and even tips on sea survival.

Horsburgh published this compilation using his own funds, and it was only after its publication he was acknowledged as an expert in this field. His decades of perseverance paid off when, after Alexander Dalrymple died, Horsburgh replaced him as the Hydrographer to the East India Company in 1810. After Horsburgh died in 1836, a group of British merchants and ships captains got together in Canton, China. They decided to build a lighthouse as a fitting memorial to him, the funding for which was to be collected from donations. A 109-foot tall lighthouse tower with black and white horizontal bands and a white flashing light was erected in 1851 at the eastern entrance to the Singapore Straits and named the Horsburgh Light. In his *India Directory*, Horsburgh provided this advice on sailing the Torres Strait:

> When the Westerly Monsoon prevails in the Timor Sea and between New Holland and New Guinea particularly in November, December, January and February, no ship should attempt to sail through the Torres Strait, either to the west or eastward as in these months dark, rainy or squally weather, would greatly augment the danger of this intricate navigation, which has seldom been attempted from the westward at any time nor from the eastward at an unfavourable season.

The first known attempt at a voyage from west to east was made by the colonial brig *Kangaroo* under the command of Lieutenant Charles Jeffries. On his return passage from Ceylon late in 1815, he waited patiently for the Westerly Monsoon to set in before trying to make Timor, the Arafura Sea, and Torres Strait. However, contrary winds thwarted his efforts, and he had to turn south-west and proceed by way of Cape Leeuwin. This whole painful and prolonged passage to Port Jackson took 25 weeks.

In 1822, Captain Peter Gordon of the colonial brig *Nimrod* planned to make the voyage from India to Sydney via the Torres Strait but only reached as far as Bali before contrary winds forced him to abandon the effort.

Captain John Lihou entered the merchant service of the British East India Company in Calcutta and commanded the ship *Zenobia* for some years in the East Indies and the Pacific. He was undoubtedly aware of James Horsburgh's advice, but he also knew January would be the best time to attempt this voyage. Either through ignorance or daring, he seemed intent on conquering the Torres Strait despite the strong tidal stream against him. The *Zenobia* entered Endeavour Strait in January 1823. She found an anchorage on the south coast of Prince of Wales Island (Muralag), which was subsequently named Port Lihou and then exited by the Murray Island Passage; this traverse of the strait called for nerves of steel with navigation and seamanship of the highest order. For safety reasons, the *Zenobia* would have to anchor at night, but the strong currents ripping through narrow channels caused the loss of all her anchors, forcing them to use her 24-pounder cannons as replacements.

After completing this first west-east passage, Captain Lihou needed to call at Port Jackson to refit and procure new anchors before continuing his voyage. The following is extracted from the Sydney Gazette, April 1823:

> The *Zenobia* in sailing from Manila to South America is the first ship, we believe, which has ever succeeded in passing Torres Straits from the westward and against the trade winds, the general course being from the eastward. This essay of nautical skill was accomplished after the loss of four anchors and later being forced to use cannon as an anchor. The ship was brought up in a fine and extensive harbour in Endeavour Strait (Port Lihou), which Captain Lihou reports to be capable of affording commodious and safe anchorage to a first-rate man-of-war, having 6½ fathoms, with a mud bottom, within a bar that crosses the entrance, but over which the Zenobia, of 550 tons, glided with ease. Here she was able to repair her rudder which

had been knocked off on a coral rock. This harbour, which had not previously been discovered by any British commander unless Captain King, R.N. should have gone in that direction, afforded plenty of excellent fresh water.

There was no rush to follow the intrepid voyage of the *Zenobia*. However, early in 1827, Captain John Grimes in the brig *Anne* planned to pass from Timor through the Torres Strait to Sydney. He managed to get as far as the Gulf of Carpentaria by late April but could not proceed further in the face of strong easterly winds, forcing him to turn back and take the southern route via Cape Leeuwin.

17

The Charles Eaton and Head-hunters in the Torres Strait, 1834

> I found the skulls of the unfortunate people on the middle of the island, covered with a kind of shed and arranged near a place where they generally feasted on the dead. These skulls of different people were placed around the head-like figure of a man painted with ochre.
>
> Captain Charles Lewis of HM colonial schooner *Isabella*, 1836

In July 1834, the barque *Charles Eaton* sailed from Sydney bound for Canton through the Torres Strait. The ship consisted of Captain Frederick Moore, the chief mate Mr Clare, the surgeon Dr Grant and twenty-three others, including two cabin boys, John Sexton and John Ireland. The passengers were an English gentleman named Armstrong and Captain D'Oyly of the Bengal Artillery, his wife, their children George (seven years old), William (two years old) and their Bengali nurse.

Sailing the Outer Passage, Captain Moore reached the approximate latitude of the Torres Strait, but since it was raining and blowing a gale, he ordered the reefing of the topgallant sails to reduce canvas and slow his vessel down. According to John Ireland, 'At daylight the next morning, we again set sail, although the wind was very high, and the water was getting rough'. There were so many heavy clouds that Moore could not possibly take a reading for latitude and it is reasonable to assume that Captain Moore had no idea where he was. But he found a gap in the surf and steered boldly for the entrance; however, it was already too late by the time he realised his error. The helmsman attempted to tack, but the barque responded slowly and continued to bear down upon the breakers with the current behind it. The *Charles Eaton* then ploughed into the reef with a splintering, sickening crunch; her keel and rudder dragged across the coral until it wrenched them off, and the sea carried the remains away. The barque fell broadside, and water broke over her decks. Fortunately, the upper part of the vessel held together, and this was where the crew and passengers collected. The cabin boy, John Ireland, described their desperate situation:

> It was happy for us that the upper part kept together as it did, though there was so much danger from the water rising, that everybody expected to be washed over. There was plainly to be heard above the din of the wind and sea, the horrible groaning of the planks forming the sides of the ship, between which the water rushed as through a sieve, and as they were broken one by one from the ill-fated vessel, we felt we were approaching nearer and nearer to a death from which we could not hope to escape, unless by some merciful interposition of Divine Goodness we should be rescued from our watery enemy.

During the confusion, one of the quarter-boats was lowered but immediately swamped, by which one crewman was drowned. Soon afterwards, the third mate, the carpenter and one of the seamen put sails, provisions, water, arms, and all the carpenter's tools into the other quarter-boat, lowered her down and reached safe water. Two seamen then risked their lives to swim through heavy breakers to join them, after which the third mate refused to take any more passengers. This quarter-boat then left those on the wreck to their fate and steered a westerly course in an attempt to reach the Dutch settlement at Kupang. After sailing for fifteen days, they reached the island of Tanimbar, where they remained for more than thirteen months until a trading vessel could take them to the Dutch settlement at Ambon and then on to Batavia in October 1835. Here, they reported to the Dutch authorities that the *Charles Eaton* had sunk near the entrance to the Torres Strait. The report from the Dutch in Batavia reads:

> We have just received some intelligence respecting the unfortunate barque *Charles Eaton,* which we hasten to impart to you. Five of the crew arrived here yesterday in a coasting vessel called the *Patriot,* commanded by Captain Clunie from Amboyna. The following is their account of the loss. It appears that, when the *Charles Eaton* was close to the entrance of Torres Straits, she mistook the entrance and, before the ship could be put about, struck on the reef, the sea breaking heavily on them at the same time when the Long Boat was instantly stove. When the five sailors left the Ship in the Jolly Boat, Captain Moore was clinging to the Main chain and a Captain D'Oyly, one of the passengers with his Lady and children, standing near him. The sailors think all remaining on board must have perished; and the sea being tremendous, the ship must have gone to pieces.

In September 1835, Captain Carr, with the trading ship *Mangles*, delivered 310 convicts to Hobart Town, then sailed directly to the Murray Islands, where he had previously traded for turtle shells to bring to the Canton market. The island was thickly covered with trees of various descriptions, with coconut plantations spreading up the lower reaches of the hills. He could see an almost unbroken line of thatched beehive-shaped huts grouped into villages along the beach. Many large outrigger canoes were drawn up on the sand, while bamboo fences protected the beachfront gardens and plantations from the monsoonal gales that regularly blew in from the sea. After anchoring near the island, several canoes came out to trade. In one of the canoes, they saw a white man, as naked as any of the islanders; on being questioned, he claimed to be an Englishman named John Ireland who had survived the wreck of the *Charles Eaton* and that other survivors were being held ashore. This news caused consternation and hope when it reached London. Captain D'Oyley had influential relatives who brought pressure to bear on the colonial authorities, who sent a ship from Sydney to investigate and rescue any survivors.

In June 1836, Captain Charles Lewis, with the colonial schooner *Isabella*, sailed from Sydney fitted out with cannon and plenty of ammunition, plus a supply of iron axes and trinkets to trade for the survivors. Everyone believed that besides the lad seen by Captain Carr, there were nine or more other survivors of the wreck. After they reached Murray Island, they found only two surviving boys – John Ireland (aged in his teens) and William D'Oyley (aged 4), whose rescue they successfully negotiated. John Ireland gave the following account of the melancholy fate of those who had remained on the wreck of the *Charles Eaton*:

> The master then, assisted by those who remained, attempted to make a raft, which was not completed before the expiration of seven days. During this interval they had managed to distil a cask and some bottles of water from the sea, by the aid of the ship's coppers, and a leaden pipe from the quarter gallery cistern, the whole of which they placed on the raft with a basket containing beer, and a cask of pork.
>
> As soon as the raft was completed, they got upon it, but finding that it was not buoyant enough to hold them, they threw over the water, the pork and beer. Still, it did not support their weight, so the greater number returned on board; leaving Captain Moore, the Master, Mr. Grant the surgeon, Mr. Armstrong, Captain and Mrs. D'Oyly, with their two children and their

nurse, also two seamen, who remained upon it all night. In the morning, however, it was found that the rope by which the raft had been fastened to the stern of the wreck had been cut and nothing was seen of their companions. It is probable that the uncomfortable situation in which they found themselves, up to their waists in water, and the sea constantly breaching over them, induced the master to cut the rope and trust Providence to guide himself and the passengers to some place of safety.

Those that remained on the wreck then made another raft of the vessel's topmasts lashed together with coir rope and made a sail out of some cloth that formed a part of her cargo. John Ireland further described that after two days and nights upon the raft, up to their waists in water, and having very little food, they passed an island and saw several more ahead. Soon afterwards, a canoe was seen paddling towards them, containing ten or twelve Islanders, who, as they approached, stood up and extended their arms to show they had no weapons and were inclined to be friendly. On reaching the raft, the Islanders then conducted them to shore.

Upon disembarking, the survivors searched for food and water, but they were so exhausted by fatigue and hunger they could scarcely crawl. Upon their return to the place where they landed, they threw themselves on the ground in despair as it was evident from the ferocious bearing and conduct of the Islanders that they had murderous intent. In this dreadful state of suspense, Mr Clare, the chief mate, recommended they be resigned to their fate and read to them, in a most impressive manner, several prayers from a book that he had brought with him from the wreck, after which, commending themselves to the protection of the Almighty, they laid down and worn out by severe exhaustion, were soon asleep. But it was for them the sleep of death because, as Ireland describes, he was roused by a shout and noise and, upon looking up, saw the Islanders murdering his companions by dashing their brains out with clubs.

The next day, the Islanders collected all the heads and moved to an island near Aureed, where the women lived. On landing there, Ireland saw the two of Captain D'Oyly's children from the first raft to leave the wreck. The elder D'Oyly told him that after they landed on this island, all the passengers, including his parents, had been murdered except himself and his young brother.

We do not know the fate of the oldest D'Oyly, but the captivity of John Ireland and the youngest D'Oyly ended when a Murray Islander named Duppar rescued them. The price of their ransom was one branch of bananas for each. On Murray Island, John Ireland lived in the same hut with Duppar and his family, where his job was to cultivate a plantation of yams and, during the season, to assist in taking turtle and shellfish. Captain Lewis said another Murray Island family showered little William with love. Known as Uass, he completely forgot his European mother and devoted himself to his new parents. Sturdy and browned by the sun, the boy spoke only the native language and cried bitterly when taken from his Murray Island home.

In a letter dated June 26, 1836, Captain Charles Lewis describes how he found the only two survivors of the *Charles Eaton*, John Ireland, the ship cabin boy and the child William D'Oyly, aged four years:

> The father and mother, and the whole of the passengers with all of the crew, were murdered by the savages on the island, which the natives call Boydang. Consequently, those are the only two living, whom I purchased from the natives for axes. These survivors have been well treated on this island of Mer; indeed these people saved and rescued them from the savages of Boydang (near Aureed), an island to the westward, which it is also my object to visit. After searching all over the straits for this mysterious island, I at last found it, and saw no inhabitants there, they having left the previous night, when the ship hove in sight of their isle. I, however, found the skulls of the unfortunate people on the middle of the island, covered with a kind of shed, and arranged near a place where they generally feasted on

the dead. These skulls of different people were placed around the head-like figure of a man painted with ochre. I observed the skulls showed great marks of violence on them all. Having satisfied myself of the truth of this detail, I set the whole of the houses on fire and also destroyed every cocoa-nut tree in the place, which those savages generally exist on. I at the same time conveyed the skulls on board and destroyed the skull-house.

The *Isabella* returned to Sydney in October 1836, where the skulls were given a Christian burial in the old Sydney Cemetery and in December 1838, an elaborate stone monument paid for by the Colonial Government was erected over the grave site.

The 1898 Cambridge Anthropological Expedition to the Torres Strait, led by Alfred Haddon, completed a study of the Islanders and published six volumes of reports from 1901 to 1935. The reports comprehensively compiled Islander culture, history, music, language, economic relations and physical characteristics. Haddon believed change was destroying traditional Island culture, and ethnographers needed to record them before their inevitable decline. These reports described how headhunting was commonly practised to enhance participants' status and increase spiritual, ritual, and totemic power in various ceremonial contexts.

Haddon described the fate of the castaways from the *Charles Eaton* as an example of *sarup* killings. Since the castaways were 'so exhausted by fatigue and hunger, that they could scarcely crawl', they were viewed by the Islanders as metaphysically unstable and as a threat by what appeared to them to be 'white zombies'. Islanders were frequently rendered insane by such an ordeal, and survivors might be considered as good as dead. According to island tradition, losing harmony with the sea was tantamount to a loss of mind and human status. Shipwrecked individuals, *sarup*, were regarded with fear as no longer fit for society. Oral history indicates that not all castaways were put to death – those who manifested full possession of their faculties or castaway strangers thought to be the reincarnation of a loved one recently deceased might be spared. Although the missionaries and colonial authority eventually put an end to *sarup*, for those on Erub, a stigma is still attached to those who survive serious trauma at sea and spiritual recovery from such an incident remains perilous.

18

The French are stranded in the Torres Strait, 1840

> A thousand times better for us to be entombed in the eternal ice of the South Pole ... rather than see all our work wiped out by a commonplace catastrophe, by an ordinary shipwreck on coral reefs such as we had encountered so many times amongst the islands of Oceania.
>
> Dumont d'Urville, *Voyage de découvertes autour du monde et à la recherche de la Pérouse. 1826-1829*

Captain Jules Dumont d'Urville was a brilliant and enigmatic sailor who commanded two great French scientific voyages to the Pacific in 1826-29 and 1837-40. By the age of 17, he was accepted into the French Navy, graduated at the top of his class, and attained the rank of Ensign three years later. He had many interests, including astronomy, geology, entomology, and botany, and was fluent in English, German, Spanish, Greek, Italian, and Hebrew.

In 1822, he served as second in command on a voyage around the world on board *La Coquille*. The expedition returned to France in 1825 with many animals and plants collected from across the Pacific.

In 1826, Dumont was given command of the *Astrolabe*, which sailed to the Pacific by way of Australia and New Zealand. The major success of this expedition was the visit to Vanikoro in the Solomon Islands, where, because of relics his divers brought up from the reefs and his questioning of the natives, Dumont found where La Perouse's ships had been lost in 1788 when they ran into the reefs surrounding the island at night. It also appeared from the native accounts and material he received that there had been survivors. The *Astrolabe* returned to Marseille in March 1829 with an impressive number of hydrographic charts and collections of zoological, botanical, and mineralogical specimens, as well as reports destined to influence the scientific analysis of those regions. By May 1835, d'Urville finished the publication of the results of this expedition, which consisted of twelve volumes and five volumes of illustrations and maps. In his reports, d'Urville first used the terms Micronesian and Melanesian, distinguishing these Pacific cultures and island groups from Polynesian.

He was then promoted to post Captain at his homeport of Toulon, but he describes how he found himself out of favour:

> For more than eighteen months I had no share in ministerial favours and I had to resign myself to carry out the obscure duties that are the lot of a ship's captain in port ... Also, I must be honest; at the beginning of the July revolution (1830), perhaps over-enthusiasm had inspired in me some very radical opinions which I did not bother to conceal. This behaviour, at the very least, unwise, in a profession where unquestioning and almost blind obedience is demanded, had brought me quite unfavourably to the notice of the Navy Ministry.

Dumont was torn between his quiet life as Port Captain in Toulon and his wish to lead another important expedition to the Pacific. Bored with his port duties and probably wishing to revive his naval career d'Urville proposed another Pacific Expedition to the Naval Ministry. By this time, the British sealer James Weddell reported in 1823 to have sailed to the most southerly latitude yet achieved at 74°34'S and interest in Antarctic exploration was renewed. D'Urville describes the response to his proposal:

> In effect, towards the end of February, I received a communication in which I was told that the King himself, to whom my plan had been submitted, had welcomed it, but having learned that an American whaling ship had got very near to the South Pole, he desired that a French expedition be sent in the same direction. Consequently, the proposal was put to me to command two ships, and I would start my expedition by pushing towards the South Pole.

European attention had now turned to Antarctica, the earth's last great unexplored area, and he had not expected to be appointed commander of a hazardous expedition to the world's southern regions. The *Astrolabe* and the *Zélée* left Toulon in September 1837, and d'Urville describes the mixed emotions of his departure and the tearful goodbye to his wife and family:

> Exactly at noon, I said goodbye to my wife and children. This was a very painful moment for me. Twice already I had undergone this cruel ordeal, but then I was young, strong, and full of hope, optimism and illusions. But in 1837 I was old (47!), subject to attacks of a cruel malady, completely disenchanted and stripped of illusions. So, I left behind all that was dearest to me in the world. I voluntarily relinquished the only happiness I could savour, once again to throw myself into a gruelling and thankless campaign which was possibly not going to offer me any real compensations. So it was that when I gave a last kiss to my Adélie, all those thoughts came to assail me and I could not hold back my tears, and I cursed my sad destiny. But it was too

late: I had filled my cup and I had to drink. I looked one last time at the walls of my humble town, then I quickly turned and went aboard.

The instructions for this expedition, dated 26 August 1837, were for the two corvettes *Astrolabe* and *Zélée* to sail for the Cape Verde Islands for reprovisioning, then head south towards the Antarctic Peninsula. After reaching the South Orkney Islands. the expedition then sailed towards the South Shetland Islands where, despite thick fog, they observed some land they sketched on their maps. Dumont was to attempt to sail across the Antarctic Circle. However, the way was blocked by pack ice. At the end of February 1838, he accepted that he could not continue further south and began to doubt the accuracy of Weddell's claim. He consequently sailed to Chile, establishing a temporary hospital for the crew members affected by scurvy. The two vessels then crisscrossed the Pacific, visiting Tahiti, Western Samoa, Fiji, the Solomon Islands, Guam, Ternate, and the Banda Islands.

The vessels left Banda in February 1839 to sail eastwards through the Torres Strait, as this was the period of the northwest monsoon when it was still theoretically possible to make this passage. This might be the first attempt to sail eastwards through the Torres Strait since the voyage of the *Zenobia* in 1823. On 9 March, they were in shallow water off False Cape in Papua. The breeze seemed steady from the west, and there was intermittent heavy rain. Anxious about being driven aground by the persistent westerly wind and currents, d'Urville delayed their entry into the Torres Strait. It was a fortunate decision because, on 11 March, the west wind swung to the east, signalling the possible end of the northwest monsoon. The next day, a persistent strong swell from the east forced d'Urville to abandon the planned easterly voyage through the Strait. Two days later, the north-westerlies came back in strength. However, any regret at abandoning the Strait was short-lived, as he wrote:

> On the 15th in the evening, the horizon looked as if it was on fire. Never in my life have I seen clouds so charged with electricity; at one point on the horizon a series of lightning flashes continually rent the clouds. It looked like a great fire from which huge rockets were shooting up, hurling their sparks into the sky. The next day, the winds still from the west, blew violently and forced us to take further reefs in the already reefed topsail. The sea became hollow and causes our poor corvettes to work. We would certainly have been wrecked if this bad weather had caught us amongst the reefs of the Torres Strait.

The vessels then conducted a tour of Southeast Asian ports to wait for the onset of the Antarctic summer and the time for another expedition to the south. From there they sailed down the west coast of Australia to Hobart, then sailed south to Antarctica. On 20 January 1840, the expedition crossed the Antarctic Circle and sighted land that same afternoon. The two ships then sailed slowly to the west while skirting ice walls until they encountered a rocky islet only a few hundred yards off the coast at 66º 37" south. Some crew members landed on the island, where they hoisted the French tricolour. Dumont named the island Dumoulin after the hydrographer of the voyage and named the land beyond Terre Adélie, after his wife. The result of this second voyage to Antarctica was that d'Urville could claim that the French had landed on the Antarctic continent ahead of the American Wilkes and the British Ross expeditions. Recording the landing and departure, officer Joseph-Fidéle-Eugéne Dobouzet wrote:

> We saluted our discovery with a general hurrah … The echoes of these silent regions, for the first time disturbed by human voices, repeated our cries and then returned to their habitual silence.

The *Astrolabe* and *Zélée* sailed to New Zealand and planned to return to France by sailing through the Torres Strait from the east. There was still a long and hazardous voyage ahead before they would reach home, but at that time of the year, the southeast winds were dependable. On 23 May 1840, they began surveying the southern islands of the Louisiade Archipelago, which had never been charted since Bougainville in 1786. D'Urville was now anxious to reach home as he was in severe pain from gout and its attendant renal and intestinal problems, but as usual, his stoic determination prevailed over his physical infirmity.

On 30 May, they sighted Portlock Reefs, which were scarcely above sea level and served as a warning before the Great Barrier Reef. The following morning, they got safely through the Bligh Entrance, easily identified from tiny Anchor Cay, which marked its southern limit and anchored for the night off Erub (Darnley Island). As it was still early afternoon, Dumont sent the naturalists and the hydrographer ashore in a boat under the command of Lieutenant Duroch, ordering special caution because the natives there had previously attacked and killed some merchantmen from the *Shah Hormuzeer* and *Chesterfield*. When the crew returned, they described their encounter with the natives:

> They do not look repulsive; they even seem to have put some thought into their adornment; one of them was wearing a woven straw headband decorated with mother-of-pearl; another was wearing on his ankles and arms bark bracelets finely worked and painted red; some of them and this was really bizarre, were wearing wigs. Their imitation of hair is so perfect that it was only by pure chance that led us to discover this ... they are well proportioned, although their legs are rather skinny. We also saw some women, with whose aid they tried to coax us inland.

The next morning, the vessels sailed southwest following the Warrior Reefs and intended to anchor at Tudu (Warrior Island) on the southerly end of the reefs. On seeing what he thought was the end of the reefs, d'Urville gave orders to bear away to starboard when disaster struck. There was a sudden and ominous jolt, and then *Astrolabe* stopped, listing slightly. The *Zélée* had executed the same manoeuvre, and grounded on the same reef before there was any chance to shout a warning. A heavy swell from the east began to buffet the corvettes; the masts were threatening to come down, and there was a risk the ships might break up under the effect of such pounding. As a result, the sails were furled, the top gallants stripped, and the ship's boats laid out anchors. They hoped they would float off with the next high tide by warping the vessels, but it made no difference. The next high tide only lifted the vessels and pushed them closer to Tudu Island. As the tide ebbed, the vessels heeled over further and further and looked like capsizing.

The Astrolabe and Zelle on the reef at Tudu Island
Louis Le Breton, Atlas Pittoresque, Australian National Maritime Museum

It seemed the expedition had come to an unfortunate end, and d'Urville wrote in despair:

> The most dismal thought went through my mind ... Our corvettes had run up thirty-four months of campaigning and it was all for nothing ... They had emerged victorious from their battles in the ice to perish miserably on a nameless reef. A

thousand times better for us to be entombed in the eternal ice of the South Pole ... rather than see all our work wiped out by a commonplace catastrophe, by an ordinary shipwreck on coral reefs such as we had encountered so many times amongst the islands of Oceania!

It is interesting to note that Louis Le Breton was the junior assistant surgeon on the *Astrolabe*. After the death of the official expedition artist in Hobart in 1840, he assumed this position and produced some beautiful lithographs and paintings. Whatever his abilities as a doctor, his artistic gifts were greater. He became a distinguished maritime artist and exhibited in the Louvre between 1841 and 1849.

The natives of Tudu, who walked along the exposed reefs to the stricken ships, were friendly and gave them a moment of grim amusement when they asked whether it would not be safer for the ships to anchor in the channel instead of resting on the reef. It was time to unload the vessels of all heavy items and move the collections, charts, and provisions to the safety of Tudu Island. The *Astrolabe* was listing so heavily that they tried vainly to prop her up, then attempted to strike the topmast to make her less top-heavy but could not succeed. Luckily, the *Zélée* freed herself on the flood tide, so at the next high tide, her sailors were able to help the *Astrolabe's* crew work the capstan and heave on the anchors in an attempt to right the ship. D'Urville conveys the drama and suspense of this moment:

> The corvette was heeling over at an angle of 32 degrees and the sea had still not reached its lowest. The carpenters, axe in hand, were at the foot of each mast, ready to chop them down to take the strain off the ship which was ready to capsize. At 9pm the wheel pendulum indicated the extreme list of 38 degrees. The water had reached the deck and in a short time would begin to fill the ship. The weather was frightful; a gale was blowing from the southeast in violent squalls with heavy rain.

But then there was a near miracle, a miracle which they did not fully understand. Slowly, slowly, the wheel pendulum indicated that the list was diminishing. In some extraordinary manner, the gale, by forcing the water back to the west, caused the sea to begin to rise before low tide, and the corvette announced by little bumps that she could be refloated. Finally afloat and moored in the channel, both crews set to repair the rigging and restore order aboard their vessels.

Before leaving, D'Urville made a few observations about Tudu Island and its population. It was a sand island, scarcely a mile long and just above sea level. It had no drinkable water, no coconuts and no food plants at all. The natives lived on fish and collected water in clam shells placed under pandanus palms to catch the run-off from leaves. They seemed gentle and shy and went to great lengths to hide their womenfolk, a possible indication of the sexual harassment they had to put up with from whaling crews or merchantmen. D'Urville was intrigued by their tombs, over which were heaped pyramids of dugong skulls and bones.

By 9 June 1840, they were ready to leave and put the Torres Strait and the memory of their grounding and near capsize behind them. It took three days to reach the open sea as they carefully sounded their way through the many channels, small islands, and reefs that dotted the Strait. They then headed to their home port, hoping there had been no major damage to the ship's hulls.

All the crew were on deck for their first sighting of France in November, and later that evening, the *Astrolabe* and the *Zélée* dropped anchor in Toulon harbour, thirty-eight months since their departure. After formalities were completed, d'Urville wrote:

> As for myself it was time to go home. My sufferings had got cruelly worse and I was in need of all the care and rest I could get, to be able, after two months, to betake myself to Paris on the orders of the Navy Minister. I immediately set to work editing the material collected during the campaign.

Saved from the embarrassment of a wreckage in the Torres Strait, Dumont d'Urville finally got the recognition he deserved. He was promoted to Rear Admiral, awarded the Gold Medal of the Société de Géographie, and later became its president. He took over the writing of the expedition report, which was published between 1841 and 1854 in 24 volumes, plus seven more volumes with illustrations and maps.

19

Hydrographic Surveys in the Torres Strait, 1837 – 1850

A large proportion of the vessels trading to the South Sea and Australia, are obliged to return to Europe, or proceed to India by way of the Torres Strait ... and stand out to sea till an opportunity offers for making one of the narrow gaps in the Barrier Reef through which they steer for the Strait, and whereas, several vessels have been lost, there being no other guide to these openings than the casual observation of latitude which is often incorrect.

Admiralty directive to the HM survey ships *Fly* and *Bramble*. 1842

A safe route through the Torres Strait became an important consideration for Britain as trade strengthened between Port Jackson, China and India. In 1837, the Royal Navy Hydrographic Service decided to continue the work of Phillip Parker King. This was the beginning of an extensive surveying program that continued for the next thirteen years. The first hydrographic survey of the Torres Strait was carried out from

1842 to 1846 by Captain Blackwood in *HM Corvette Fly*, accompanied by Lieutenant Yule in the tender *Bramble*.

On 1 August 1843, the *Fly* anchored near where the *Pandora* was lost in 1791 on her return from Tahiti. From this location, Blackwood had to decide the best way of entering the Torres Strait from the Coral Sea. He opted for a passage near Raine Island, which lay at the entrance to one of the widest and clearest openings through the Great Barrier Reef . Blackwood thought it was here that ships sailing the Outer Route could pass through the Reef, enter the Inner Route and proceeding cautiously could safely traverse the Torres Strait in a few days, provided they took the precaution of anchoring during the night. Raine Island is a low-lying coral platform devoid of trees or any scrub. It is 800 metres long, 400 metres wide, and only a few metres above sea level. According to Captain Blackwood:

> A ship intending to enter the Barrier by the passage of Raine's Island, should shape a course so as to make the southern extreme of a large detached horse-shoe Reef in lat. 11° 50′ S., long. 144° 11′E . . . Having sighted the breakers, which may be safely approached within a short mile, a north course will be steered along the outer edge of this detached reef, when this distance being run, Raine's Island will be seen, and a N. W. by N. course should be shaped for it.

The Tower at Raine Island
Edwin Augustus Porcher, National Library of Australia

In May 1844, the cutter *Prince George* arrived at Raine Island with 20 convict masons. They built a tower on the island, which was 23 metres high and consisted of three levels, with walls 3 metres thick and a domed roof made of timbers recovered from the numerous wrecks on the reef. It seems the tower was of questionable value as a landmark, especially in difficult weather, as more than twenty ships were wrecked in the vicinity over the following fifteen years. However, survivors found shelter in the tower on Raine Island within its three-storied accommodation, and the island's bird population provided a ready food source for castaways.

William Bligh was the first to officially suggest a refuge for seamen in distress at the western end of the Torres Strait. It was not until 1824, however, that a depot stocked with food and water was established on Booby Island. Another function of the Booby Island depot was that of a Post Office. Passing ships would leave mail in a steel box in the 'Post Office Cave' and pick up those letters they could convey to the correct destination. Most passing vessels would anchor off the island, the dangers of Torres Strait having been passed, and record their names in the logbook. Examination of the logbook found that most of the vessels had taken the Outer Passage and entered at Raine Island, thus demonstrating the benefit of the Raine Island Beacon and the common use of this passage.

'The Narrative of the Surveying Voyage of H.M.S. Fly, commanded by Captain F. P. Blackwood, R.N. 1842-46', was written by Joseph Jukes, the naturalist for the expedition. Jukes had gone to Cambridge to study for a clerical career, and like Charles Darwin, he had been seduced by the extra-curricular fascinations of geology. In his narrative, he was the first to give a general account of the Torres Strait's physical geography, geology, flora and fauna, and the peoples of the Eastern Islands.

Perhaps because of his clerical training and his position as a naturalist, Jukes felt much more empathy towards the Torres Strait Islanders than his British Navy compatriots, who had been trained to see the Islanders as a threat. In contrast, it took Jukes only hours to warm to the good-natured spirits he met on the beach holding up coconuts and shouting *"poud, poud, poud* – peace, peace, peace" as they advanced. The young people remembered him, yelling out his nickname 'Jookie' when they saw him. Everything Jukes observed seemed to contradict the islanders' reputation for savagery, as he was impressed by the simple villages studded with fine houses, cultivated gardens of yams and plantains, magnificent twin-hulled sailing canoes; the elaborate collections of crafts, fabrics, carvings, weapons and trade goods. He described the islanders on Erub as follows:

> The men were fine active well-made fellows, rather above middle height, of a dark brown or chocolate colour. They had frequently almost handsome faces, aquiline noses rather broad about the nostril, well-shaped heads, and many had a singular Jewish cast of features. A look common amongst the Kiwais of Papua, so originally the Eastern Islands must have been of similar racial stock.
>
> The women wore skirts made of pandanus, had tattoos about the arms and chest, and wore close-cropped hair. The men wore long hair which was arranged in ringlets down to their shoulders, sometimes smeared with red ochre and decorated with brightly coloured feathers. The men of Erub, like those of Mer, wore no clothing. Both men and women hung pearl shells around their necks and perforated their ears.

Hut and Natives of Darnley Island
H.S. Melville, National Library of Australia

In a letter to his sister, Jukes summed up the prevailing attitude of the crew towards the islanders:

> Altogether we have been greatly interested and amused with these people and like them much; no fault could be found with them were it not that they have an unfortunate predilection for collecting skulls ... from an idea that all the skulls they can collect during the lifetime of the owners shall be their servants and followers in the next world. Of course, to have a white man as a slave would be a great honour.

As the vessels sailed north from Erub towards the unknown and previously unchartered Papuan coast, the excitement was high. The most significant of their discoveries was made when, in early June, the mouth of a huge river was explored and charted. It was named the Fly River, and Jukes realised the river's potential when he wrote, 'A small light steamer, drawing six feet of water might probably penetrate for a couple of hundred miles, into the very heart of this unexplored country'.

On the *Fly*'s third cruise, the northeast entrance into Torres Strait, known as the Bligh Entrance, was surveyed. This 16-mile-wide passage was clear of sunken dangers, averaged between nine and 12 fathoms in depth and good anchorages were available all along the passage. It would be possible to follow this course through Torres Strait even during the monsoon season, and it soon superseded the passage from Raine Island into Torres Strait for those sailing the Outer Reef.

The surveys made by the *Fly* and *Bramble* were followed in 1846 by Captain Owen Stanley in the frigate HMS *Rattlesnake*. With Yule still in command, the Bramble became the *Rattlesnake*'s tender. Between 1846 and 1850 these two ships carried out surveys of the Torres Strait, the Louisiade Archipelago and eastern New Guinea and extended the earlier work of Blackwood. Notable members of the *Rattlesnake*'s company included assistant surgeon Thomas Huxley, the later influential supporter of Darwinism, the artist Oswald Brierly and the zoologist John MacGillivray formerly of the *Fly*. The *Rattlesnake* continued the work of the *Fly* in Torres Strait by charting the western channels, including the Prince of Wales Channel and the Endeavour Strait.

Painting of HMS Rattlesnake
Oswald Brierly, 1849, Australian National Archives.

This painting by Oswald Brierly shows HMS *Rattlesnake* and its tender, HMS *Bramble*, off New Guinea. What is significant is the depiction of three types of Islander watercraft: a simple dugout canoe with an elaborately carved prow, possibly representing a dugong; a larger single-outrigger with sewn planks at the bow to raise its height; and, in the background, what are possibly three double-hulled outrigger canoes with a mast, matt sail, and platform with men standing.

Captains departing Port Jackson for the Torres Strait had to make an important decision. Whether to sail northwards to Cape York via the Inner Route between the east coast and the western edge of the Great Barrier Reef or to follow an Outer Route in the open sea beyond the eastern edge of the Great Barrier Reef. Both the Inner and Outer Routes had their advocates. The Outer Route was faster, but the Inner Route was generally considered the safest. Ships following the Outer Route could proceed at all hours without anchoring, but they could encounter uncharted coral reefs such as Wreck Reef. They then had to find a safe passage through the Great Barrier Reef when the whole swell of the South Pacific Ocean, propelled by the continual force of the trade winds, crashed onto its outer edge.

The Inner Route was 200 miles shorter than the Outer Route. The water was smooth, and shelter was better during the monsoon season. However, unmarked reefs and sandbanks were abundant, regular soundings were required in daylight, and the voyage took longer as it was necessary to anchor at night.

Captain Blackwood weighed up the merits and demerits of the two main routes towards Torres Strait. Recognising that opinions were divided on which was the preferred passage, Blackwood noted that the Inner Route was the safest, while the Outer Route was faster.

By the 1860s, the Admiralty Charts produced by these thirteen years of hydrographic surveys showed most of the hazards for vessels, enabling them to determine their passage through the Torres Strait via either the Inner or Outer Route and then follow the narrow passages and channels across the Torres Strait. However, Joseph Jukes's narrative of the *Fly*'s cruises candidly pointed out the problems of sailing through Torres Strait despite the Admiralty charts:

> However complete and accurate may be the surveys of Torres Strait and the Coral Sea it must always remain a dangerous navigation. Slight accidents, such as hazy weather, mistakes in the reckoning, unknown errors in the chronometer or sextant, a want of completeness or soundness in the rigging or finding of the vessel (to say nothing of carelessness or incapacity in the navigator), will always cause a pretty high average of wrecks in the vessels passing through Torres Strait.

20

The Rescue of Barbara Thompson, 1849

I am a white woman, why do you leave me?

Barbara Thompson, Muralag, 1849

William Thompson was a former convict who, although given a conditional pardon, was always looking for his main chance. This appeared when a former crewmember told him about a whaler wrecked on the Bampton Shoal with a cargo of whale oil. To salvage this whale oil, he left Brisbane in 1844 with some comrades and his teenage bride, Barbara, in a small cutter named *America*. It appears that the crewmember he had enlisted in this enterprise could not find the wreck, and after much quarrelling, they made their way into Torres Strait. Two crew members were lost when waves breached their overloaded dinghy and sank. Then, off the south coast of Prince of Wales Island (Muralag), the cutter was driven onto a reef during a storm. William Thompson and the one remaining crewmember were lost in attempting to swim ashore through the surf. When the gale subsided, Barbara Thompson was rescued by a party of natives, who brought her ashore.

An islander named Boroto took possession of Barbara as his share of the plunder taken from the *America*. She was compelled to live with him and a curious circumstance secured for her the protection of one of the principal men of the tribe. This person, named Piaquai, acting upon the belief that white people are the ghosts of the aborigines, fancied that in Barbara, he recognised his long-lost daughter. The whole tribe immediately acknowledged her as one of their own, and she lived with the Kaurareg community in Muralag for four to five years.

It was in October 1849 when HMS *Rattlesnake*, while surveying the region of Evans Bay near Cape York, encountered a white woman. As described by Oswald Brierly:

> About 1pm, I had gone ashore with some of the crew to amuse ourselves in a sport of recreational shooting. As we washed in preparation for our return, a number of sailors came hurrying towards us, crying out with considerable urgency that the blacks had brought a white woman down to the beach. Although I could not immediately see her since she was surrounded by our crew and supportive natives, I am told that on her initial discovery she was wearing only 'a narrow fringe of leaves in front' and no clothing.

When first seen, she presented so dirty and wretched an appearance that some of the sailors at first mistook her for an aboriginal woman and passed by without taking further notice. She then called out to them in English: "I am a white woman; why do you leave me?" Her skin was tanned and blistered with the sun and showed the marks of several large burns which had been received from sleeping too near the fire on cold nights; she was also suffering from ophthalmia, which had deprived her of the sight of one eye. Mr Scott, the coxswain, attended to common decency by dressing her in not one, but two shirts, given by the gaping sailors and as described by Barbara Thompson:

> Someone took hold of my hand and led me along to where the men were washing. He was like a guard to me. I could not understand the other men as I could him. When we reached the washing place, he took me into the bush and with another man ... washed me, combed my hair, and dressed me in two shirts, one below as a petticoat, the other over my shoulders. I was so ashamed when I got to the washing place that I did not notice what men were there. But this Scott was a friend of all of them. He took hold of me so brave like. As I went along, I could hardly speak for crying.

They learned her name was Barbara Thompson, and her tribal name was Giom. Captain Owen Stanley welcomed the young woman despite his trepidations about having her on the ship. He fed her, gave her a cabin segregated from the rest of the sailors and had the doctor tend to her burns and infected eye. To retain some order on the ship, he made it clear that Mrs Thompson would in future dine only with him and the artist Oswald Brierly, who wrote:

> Captain Stanley allowed Mrs Thompson the privacy of his own workroom to serve as her cabin. This cabin was likewise my workroom, so we found ourselves placed in close proximity ... Only then did I begin to appreciate the quick intelligence and resourcefulness of this remarkable woman ... Myself having no duty aboard the ship, I could divert what I chose to writing down her accounts and employ a larger part of everyday to writing down whatever she remembered of her island life and the customs of the natives.

Brierly knew this was a unique opportunity. Barbara could give him an accurate description of native life and culture. Her greatest knowledge, naturally, was of the women's everyday work patterns and social relations. She recounted their modes of childbirth and childcare and described their methods of making baskets, mats, grass skirts and fish traps using the leaves of the pandanus tree. She listed their methods of treating illness with bush medicines. She explained the intricate network of kinship structure and family relationships, outlining taboos and norms and the more mundane interactions between husbands, wives, children, and lovers. The island of Muralag, with its rocky soil and scrubby vegetation, made foraging challenging for the Kaurareg women. During the dry season from June to October, when the southeast trade winds prevailed, turtles, fruits and fish were relatively abundant, the clan would travel to other islands and mainland spots where the men would hunt and the women would search for yams and shellfish. Bladders of turtle oil were mixed with crushed yams to make a much-prized mash called *mabouchie*. In each camp, the women would dig large ovens, lining them with stones, for cooking turtles and dugongs. They then carved and arranged the food for distribution according to age, status and gender. During the wet season, they would crouch in long, narrow huts, enduring weeks of incessant tropical rain, while gathering nearby sources of edible mangrove pods, which the women would prepare in a mash mixed with wild beans. She gave Brierly glimpses of the secret rituals of boyhood initiations, sorcerer curses and magic. She explained the skills of canoe building and sailing, weapon making and ornamentation, fire clearing and yam cultivation, trapping fish in stone weirs and creek nets. Barbara described in detail the clan's elaborate death and mortuary rituals. She recounted myths of the Kaurareg's origins, rich in foundational stories that blended human and animal elements.

While waiting aboard the *Rattlesnake*, she was, according to Brierly, still a great favourite with the blacks and hardly a day passed on which she was not obliged to hold a reception of friends from ashore, while other visitors, less favoured, were content to talk to her through the porthole. During the nine weeks she lived onboard the *Rattlesnake*, the Muralag women brought her daily gifts of cooked turtle eggs and yams while begging her to return to the island. Oswald Brierly described one such visit from her tribal mother Gameena:

She showed the greatest joy at seeing Mrs T. and stood up in the canoe till she might take hold of her hand, which she kissed with great affection, at the same time showing a shell which had belonged to Mrs.T while on land ... in which she had bored a hole and now wore around her neck as a remembrance, saying "Giom this is yours" and at the same time kissing it.

According to Barbara Thompson, her 'husband', Boroto, was an esteemed turtle hunter with prized expertise in making magic to entice green turtles to the surface. He was also a skilled boatman, a successful trader, and one of the only three men on Muralag who owned a yam garden. He pleaded continually with Barbara for her to leave the *Rattlesnake* and return to the island, prompting the naturalist Jock MacGillivray to write:

> Her friend Boroto, the nature of the intimacy with whom was not at first understood, attempted in vain by smooth words and fair promises to induce her to go back with him, then left the ship in a rage, and we were not sorry to get rid of so impudent and troublesome a visitor as he had become. Previous to leaving, he had threatened that, should he or any of his friends catch his faithless spouse on shore, they would take off her head to carry back with them to Muralag; and so likely to be fulfilled did she consider this threat, being in perfect accordance with their customs, that she never afterwards ventured onshore at Cape York.

Captain Stanley felt it necessary to ask whether she preferred remaining with the *Rattlesnake* or accompanying the natives back to their island, as she would have free choice. She was so much agitated as to find difficulty in expressing her thankfulness, using scraps of English alternately with the Kaurareg language, and then realising she was not understood, beating her forehead with her hand as if to assist in collecting her scattered thoughts. At length, she found the words to say: "Sir, I am a Christian and would rather go back to my own friends."

Over the long weeks of the return voyage to Sydney, Barbara talked to Oswald Brierly nearly every day, and he wrote down everything she could tell him about her time with the Kaurareg people. In 1849, this was a significant insight into the traditional way of life of the indigenous people of the islands, and he wrote:

> Although perfectly illiterate, Barbara Thomson had made good use of her powers of observation and evinced much shrewdness in her remarks upon various subjects connected with her residence among the blacks, joined to great willingness to communicate any information which she possessed. Much of this will be found in another part of this volume, incorporated with the result of my own observations. Several hundred words of the Kaurareg language, and a portion of its grammar, were also obtained from time to time, and most of these were subsequently verified.

A pact of confidentiality between Brierly and Barbara would partly explain another puzzle, which is why the redemptive story of her life with the islanders in the Torres Strait sank into oblivion after the *Rattlesnake* berthed in Sydney in early February 1850. It seems that Captain Owen Stanley, Oswald Brierly and the crew of the *Rattlesnake* had agreed on a conspiracy of silence that managed to keep Barbara Thompson out of the news and protect her from the newsmen who would make her re-entry into white society a more painful affair. Brierly did not allow his notes of her to be published until after his death and little is known about her later life.

The command of a survey vessel, charting uncharted waters in a hazardous environment, can be incredibly stressful, and one of Owen Stanley's charts of Torres Strait contained more than 40,000 depth soundings. The work needed to record these readings was so demanding that Owen Stanley hardly ever left the chart room. Consequently, his health deteriorated. Gaunt and haggard, he had a paralytic seizure soon after leaving the Torres Strait. He was clearly ill on his return to Sydney and was only 38 years old when he was found dead in his cabin on 13 March 1850 while the ship lay at anchor. Thomas Huxley later wrote:

> Care and anxiety, joined to the physical debility produced by the enervating climate of New Guinea, fairly wore him out ... but he died in harness, the end attained, the work that lay before him honourably done. Which of us may dare ask for more? He has raised an enduring monument in his works, and his epitaph shall be the grateful thanks of many a mariner threading his way among the mazes of the Coral Sea.

21

The Founding of Port Albany and Somerset, 1864

> Council is convinced that steamship and telegraphic communications via Torres Strait is only a matter of time. The operation of the proposed line of steamers would be facilitated by a settlement at Cape York which could be used as a coaling station and port of call.
>
> Executive Council, Government of Queensland, 1862

In 1851, the British Government awarded mail contracts to the P&O Steam Navigation Company to bring passengers and mail from Britain to Melbourne and Sydney via Calcutta and Singapore. Onward passengers and mail for Brisbane had to be transhipped by small coastal ships. Very few British immigrants landing in Melbourne or Sydney made their way to Queensland, which was desperately short of labour in the second half of the nineteenth century.

After Queensland became a separate colony from New South Wales in 1859, establishing a direct link from Singapore to Brisbane was obviously in its interest. This would require a port and a coaling station somewhere in the Torres Strait, and the Admiralty's instructions to the survey vessel *Rattlesnake* was for it to seek a suitable location. The report reads:

> One of the more immediate beneficial results of our survey of the Inner Passage, would be to facilitate its use by steamers, should arrangements at present be contemplated for the continuance of the overland communication by Great Britain and India, from Singapore to the Australian colonies, by way of Torres Strait, ever be carried into effect, so it was of importance to find some place in the neighbourhood of Cape York, convenient as a coaling station during either monsoon. An eligible spot for this purpose was found in Port Albany, the name given by Lieutenant Yule, who surveyed it in 1846, to the narrow channel separating Albany Island from the mainland. Here, a small sandy bay with a sufficient depth of water close inshore was, after a minute examination by Captain Owen Stanley, considered to be well adapted to the running out of a jetty, alongside which the largest steamer could lie in perfect safety. This little bay has anchorage close inshore for three or four vessels only, as a little further out they would be in the stream of the tide which runs with great strength, especially in the neighbourhood of the various points; however, it is completely sheltered from any wind which may be experienced on this part of the coast.

The advantage of establishing Port Albany would be that steamships bringing mail and passengers to Brisbane might be supplied with coal, water and stores, such as the anchors frequently lost during the passage of the Strait. In 1860, the Queensland Governor began urging that a settlement be established there after the merchant vessel *Sapphire* was wrecked in Torres Straits, and all survivors were thought to have perished. Obviously, a settlement at Cape York would provide a port of refuge much closer than Timor in the event of a shipwreck.

The Queensland Governor-General, Sir George Bowen visited Cape York in 1862 with Commodore Burnett in *HMS Pioneer* and became even more firmly convinced that a settlement was necessary as a harbour of refuge for distressed seamen. It was also believed that such a port and a contingent of marines would reduce the outrages that Islanders had committed against shipwreck survivors. Eager to emulate the achievements of Thomas Stamford Raffles when he had established the port of Singapore, Bowen anticipated that at Port Albany, there would be a convergence of Asian and Pacific trade routes and that a properly garrisoned settlement would command the whole of the commerce between the Indian Ocean and the South Pacific. The Queensland Government made its intentions quite clear in July 1862 when the Executive Council stated:

> Council is convinced that steamship and telegraphic communications via Torres Strait is only a matter of time. The operation of the proposed line of steamers would be facilitated by a settlement at Cape York which could be used as a coaling station and port of call.

On 25th March 1863, the initial group of settlers, led by John Jardine, landed in the Albany Passage and began clearing land on the mainland for the settlement. A town was to be located at Somerset Point on an elevated site described as having abundant pasture, timber, good soil, and freshwater. The high ground was selected for the Police Magistrate's house, and the south-eastern slope of Somerset Point, facing the bay, was to be the site of the Marines' barracks. John Jardine was appointed Police Magistrate and Commissioner for Crown Lands at the settlement, a position he had previously held as the Rockhampton Police Magistrate, where he was already known for his bloody, vigilante justice against the Aborigines. Great difficulty was encountered in clearing the dense vine scrub, but work was underway only a month after the party's arrival. On 14 July 1864, *HMS Salamander* left Brisbane with a detachment of Royal Marines on board and accompanied by a merchant vessel bringing civilians, stores, supplies and the framework for the buildings prepared in Brisbane under the supervision of the Colonial Architect. The merchant vessel also carried 252 sheep which were landed on Albany Island.

After their father was posted to Somerset, Jardine's sons Frank and Alexander overlanded a herd of stock on a trek of 2000 km towards the Cape York Peninsula and Somerset. Accompanied by four Europeans and four Aboriginals, they left Rockhampton on 14 May 1864 with 42 horses and 250 cattle. Forcing their way through jungles, scrub, swamps and crossing at least six large rivers, they were continually harassed by aboriginals. At the Mitchell River on 13 December, they withstood a major aboriginal attack. The aborigines on Cape York obviously preferred beefsteak to kangaroo meat and the Jardines struggled to preserve their livestock. After an epic journey lasting seven months, they finally reached Somerset, clad in tatters, wearing hats of emu skin and with only 12 horses and 50 cattle remaining.

In September 1865, tenders were called for service by steamships of not less than 600 tons from Brisbane through the Inner Route to ports west of the Torres Strait, as the government may nominate. The vessel *Souchays* commenced the first voyage in January 1866, leaving Brisbane for Batavia with 20 boxes of mail and no other cargo. However, after two voyages, she had failed to improve the mail service to England and was considered too slow. She was replaced by the *Hero*, who completed three voyages and substantially improved the mail service for the new Torres Strait Mail Line. The *Hero* also demonstrated the problems with the port of Somerset as a safe coaling station because she lost two anchors while trying to hold a secure mooring.

At this time, the settlement consisted of a Police Magistrate, a Naval Surgeon, eleven marines, and a squatter occupying some wooden buildings on the west side of Albany Pass. A recent altercation meant that no natives were allowed in the settlement. An aboriginal had been falsely accused of stealing a hatchet from the settlement and had been punished. The following day, his tribe assembled to avenge the insult, and the Europeans at the settlement were attacked. Two marines had been speared, and one of them died later from his wounds. After some days, the Europeans retaliated, and five aboriginal men and one lad were shot.

On 8 February 1867, two missionaries landed at Somerset to begin evangelising the aborigines of Cape York and of the islanders of the Torres Strait. At the time of their arrival, the Police Magistrate had ordered that no aborigines would be allowed on the settlement site, which would make any hope of evangelisation of the aborigines almost impossible, leading to this comment by one of the church missionaries:

> The aborigines have been described as the most degraded, treacherous and bloodthirsty beings in existence by the present Police Magistrate and those whose only idea is to shoot them down whenever they are seen.

In 1869, John Jardine applied for a leave of absence, and Henry Chester was appointed to succeed him. In his autobiography, Chester wrote:

> On arrival at Somerset, I found the garrison to consist of a sergeant and four town police constables, with five native troopers. One of the constables, a married man, looked after the troopers and lived on the southern hill. There were seventeen horses and a mob of about a hundred cattle running in the bush. Jardine remained for a week and showed me over the Settlement. He impressed on me never on any account to leave the house without carrying a revolver even if only going as far as the stockyard and cautioned me, in the event of a night attack by the aborigines, never to stand upright on the veranda where the aborigines could see me but to go on my hands and knees, the better to see them.

John Jardine's trip back to Brisbane shows an example of the difficulties of transport from Somerset. Jardine left in the schooner that brought Chester to Somerset. Captain Hannah attempted to beat down the coast against the South-East trade winds, but after nearly three weeks, had to give it up and run back before the wind to Somerset, from where they sailed through the Torres Strait, then around the south coast of Australia, and after three months finally reached Brisbane.

The Queensland Colony recognised the strategic importance of the Torres Strait and moved to secure it under its jurisdiction in August 1872, when the British Government issued letters to extend the boundary of the colony to encompass all islands within a 60-nautical mile radius of the coast of Queensland. This meant that the northern islands, including Saibai, Boigu and Dauan, and the eastern island of Mer, were left outside the boundary and came under the nominal control of the Governor of Fiji and the British Western Pacific High Commission.

The opening of the Suez Canal in 1869 renewed interest in a mail steamship line between Asian ports and Queensland. In May 1873, the Eastern and Australian Mail Steam Company was registered and received a Queensland Government contract to provide a mail service through the Torres Strait between Brisbane and Singapore. The maiden voyage was made by a ship called the *Sun Foo*, and pilotage through the Inner Route was provided by a shipmaster familiar with the route. This service was later extended to Hong Kong and settled into a regular sailing pattern with mail, passengers and cargo.

However, the settlement at Somerset had encountered serious problems, voracious white ants were eating the buildings with relish, and hostile local aborigines were attacking the cattle and sheep. The anchorage in Albany Passage was regarded as very troublesome and even dangerous for large mail steamers. The strong tides racing through the channel created significant problems for ships mooring, and they often had to hold on with both anchors. Because of these problems, the dream of a new Singapore proved to be an illusion, and the settlement languished. Captain Moresby of the *HMS Basilisk* made a blunt assessment of Somerset in a report in 1873:

> I am of the opinion Somerset has failed and is most unsuitably placed for fulfilling the original objectives of its establishment.

Moresby went on to describe, in unflattering detail, the port's degeneration. Buildings were unpainted and ravaged by white ants. Government equipment and supplies deteriorated rapidly due to the climate and neglect. Fencing and stockyards were broken down and rotting. Jardine's cattle were to be encountered running wild up to 100 kilometres away. It was a decaying settlement often frequented by a rough assortment of pearlers, bêche-de-mer collectors and 'blackbirders' providing Pacific labourers.

As a port of refuge, Somerset was far from ships sailing the Outer Route and the North East Channel. Nevertheless, in the thirteen years before its abandonment by the government in 1877, the survivors of fourteen shipwrecks had found refuge there and 85 people were saved. Henry Chester used the case of the three-masted North German schooner *Honolulu* as an argument for moving the settlement to the Prince of Wales group of islands. The *Honolulu* was seen aground on an unknown reef in the North East Channel of Torres Straits by the master of the barque *Loch Awe* on 20 July 1870. The ship was within 30 miles of the harbour of refuge at Somerset, but they had received no news of the wreck. Henry Chester first heard of the incident on 19 October when the brig *Western Star* arrived at Somerset with a Sydney newspaper containing the news, which had reached Sydney from Batavia. In his report to the President of the Marine Board in Brisbane, Chester stated that for every vessel passing within sight of Somerset, ten used the North East Channel, making Somerset ineffectual as a harbour of refuge.

The Prince of Wales group of islands, lying between the only two navigable channels through the Torres Strait, was the logical place to move the settlement. It was now only a matter of deciding which day of the week to choose for the site of the new settlement – Wednesday, Thursday, or Friday. William Bligh had named Wednesday Island and Owen Stanley followed this theme by giving the names of Thursday and Friday to the other islands in the group. After several government visits, a site was chosen for the new settlement at the western end of Thursday Island. Accordingly, in December 1876, a proclamation was made declaring Thursday Island (Waiben) a government reserve for public purposes.

22

Pearls and Priests, 1860-1914

> We bless you for your having brought that Resurrection light to those who lived in the Torres Strait Islands in 1871 through the London Missionary Society.
>
> Anglican Board of Mission

Trepang (Sea Cucumber or bêche-de-mer) is a marine invertebrate prized in the Chinese market for its culinary value and medicinal properties. It had first been gathered in Australia by the Macassans from the Indonesian island of Sulawesi, who followed the trade winds to the Kimberly and Arnhem coasts to set up annual settlements for the collection and processing of trepang. All that was required to collect them was to walk over the reefs and sand flats at low tide to gather up the sea slugs, and aboriginal labour was conscripted for this purpose. The trepang is then placed in boiling water before being dried and smoked to preserve the catch until it reaches Asian markets. Even before the settlement of Somerset, a Captain Edwards had an operation on Albany Island collecting and smoking trepang for the Chinese market.

In the 1860s, Captain William Banner established a station on Tudu Island where he employed some Kanakas (Pacific Islanders) to collect and process the trepang for export to Asia. Towards the beginning of 1870, Captain Banner sailed for Sydney with his cargo of trepang, leaving the station in charge of a Tongan man named John Joseph. During the Captain's absence, the Tudu men took the Kanakas to a part of Warrior Reef, where they collected pearl-shell for their decoration. This was the highly valued golden-tipped *Pinctada Maxima*. When Banner returned, he immediately sensed he was onto a bonanza as pearl shell was in demand for making cutlery handles, buttons, buckles, jewellery and inlay. Six tons of shell had already been collected and this was sent to Sydney in the brig *Pakeha*. By mid-October, they had collected another fifty tons, and the shell was then shipped to Sydney in the *Bluebell* and *Pakeha*, where it was worth three to four hundred pounds a ton. Although the collection of these shells is commonly known as pearling, pearls are rarely found in shells, and their discovery provides a bonus to the lucky finder.

The crew of a pearling lugger usually consisted of two divers, two tenders (whose duty was to watch and supply air to the divers), a cook, an engineer and two deckhands. The crew were paid 40% of the earnings, and the rest went to the owner of the lugger. Earnings usually depended on the weather, crew, luck, and initiative in finding shell beds. Diving was a dangerous occupation, and many divers lost their lives due to air hoses and lifelines getting snagged on coral ledges, engines being too underpowered to fight the strong currents, or divers getting the 'bends' due to surfacing too quickly. Many divers are known to have died of the 'bends', and at no time did the islands possess a decompression chamber.

Image of Pearl Shell
Australian National Maritime Museum

In the next twenty years, fleets of schooners and luggers with their multinational crews and divers expanded across the Torres Strait and Northern Australia. The arrival of these newcomers affected every aspect of traditional island life and customs. Increasingly it was Pacific Islanders, known as Kanakas, who were brought to the islands, often as indentured labourers, to collect pearl shell. There was a tendency for these men after discharge to take land and a wife on a nearby island and settle there.

These men followed agricultural practices they had learned in the Pacific Islands, and their improved gardens included sweet potatoes, corn, and new banana types, which revolutionised those island societies that were previously semi-nomadic. These newcomers had a direct impact on the Islanders, who readily adopted their style of house, cuisine, music, and dance. Their language, Pacific Pidgin or Torres Strait Broken (Yumpla Tok), is commonly spoken today and every islander learns it as a first or second language.

On 27 June 1872, the 'Kidnapping Act' passed by the British Parliament sought to regulate the controversial labour trade from the Pacific – a part of which was related to North Queensland and the Torres Strait. It stipulated that all British labour vessels must apply for licences and pay a bond of five hundred pounds to prevent the kidnapping and mistreatment of Kanaka labour. Six months later, Captain Moresby in *HMS Basilisk* detained two schooners in Papuan waters east of the Torres Strait, which had eighty-eight South Sea Islanders on board, of whom many claimed to have been kidnapped.

The booming pearl shell trade caused the Torres Strait to become a melting pot of races, with Pacific Islanders, Japanese, Malay, and Filipinos being the main nationalities employed in the industry. The influx of Japanese into the industry began from 1885 onwards. They gradually became the principal operators as captain-divers, tenders and crew, working the luggers under contract with Australian pearling companies. The luggers, some up to 60 feet in length, were fine sea boats, as they had to withstand changes in the weather and sudden storms.

In May 1871 the vessel *Surprise* anchored off Erub (Darnley Island) with members of the London Missionary Society onboard. Its leaders, Rev. S. MacFarlane and Rev. A. Murray, had brought eight native

Deacons from the Loyalty Islands in the South Pacific. The Mission Society began the construction of wood and coral-lime cement buildings for the Papuan Institute, which would have a joint theological and manual construction curriculum. The Missionaries did not try to significantly change the unique Torres Strait Island culture as Christian principles were already somewhat compatible with the Islander religion, as a prayer to God and a conversation with the ancestors can be considered as much the same thing. Rather, they could use the Deacons from the South Pacific to introduce the Christian Gospel to the Islanders, which, by most accounts, was a much more positive approach. The idea was never to make Torres Strait Islanders into English-style Christians but for them to be enlightened by the light of Christ and his gospel of peace and love.

Known as 'The Coming of the Light', the London Missionary Society teachers quickly won the nominal support of the Islander communities to follow Christian morality and adopt Western customs of justice and administration. Also, since the pearling industry had grossly exploited the Torres Strait Islanders, the missionaries provided them with some protection and assistance. The introduction of Pacific Islanders as pastors profoundly affected customary practices. Their influences can still be seen in the Torres Strait's music, dance, art, and religion. Introduced Christian hymns tended to replace traditional sacred music, but later, locally composed sacred songs became important in worship, and there is now a rich repertoire of sacred music in the traditional languages as well as English.

The churchmen of the London Missionary Society saw themselves as answerable to their directors in London, not to the government administration on Thursday Island, with whom they were often in conflict, or to the colonial government in Brisbane. An increasing antagonism led to their withdrawal in 1914 when they handed over their responsibilities to the Anglican Church to concentrate on their evangelical mission in Papua.

On the evening of Friday, March 3, 1899, observers on Thursday Island saw an inky blackness in the eastern sky. There was a serious storm in the far distance, as lightning flashed across the sky, and if the storm struck the island, it could be disastrous. The distant storm was Cyclone Mahina, which had formed in the Coral Sea and was heading west. Fortunately, it now turned south to follow the eastern coastline of the Cape York Peninsula. Further south in Princess Charlotte Bay and Bathurst Bay near Cape Melville, many Torres Strait pearling fleet vessels were finishing their week's work and preparing for their customary Sunday break. That Saturday night, the steady breeze turned into a menacing gale as Cyclone Mahina passed overhead. Flashes of lightning lit the sea, the wind churned the waters of the bay, tearing at the ship's sails, masts, anchors, and wave after wave hit the vessels. The winds drove a huge storm surge ashore, estimated at 13 metres high, which swept 5 kilometres inland. By daybreak, Cyclone Mahina's fury had been spent, and rescue operations commenced, but the pearling fleet no longer existed. Fifty-three luggers and three hundred crewmen had been lost in the deadliest cyclone in Australia's recorded history, and only thirty survivors were found alive. For his book *The Devil's Eye*, Ian Townsend has researched the records for the names and nationalities of some of these men. He found 260 recorded deaths, of whom 77 were Japanese, 64 were Malay (Malaysia, Singapore and Indonesia), 41 were South Sea Islanders, 33 were Filipino, 15 were Aboriginal, 13 were European, 11 were Torres Strait Islanders, and six were Indian or Ceylonese. Tragically, this gave us a good idea of the multiracial composition of the pearling fleet.

Cross-cultural contact between the Islanders, Papuans and Aboriginals had always existed through an exchange of commodities. But with the newcomers, the Europeans, the Pacific Islanders, the Japanese, the Malays, the Filipinos, the Missionaries and a Colonial Administration – the social, economic, religious and political fabric of the Torres Strait and Islander life was changed forever.

23

Thursday Island and the Torres Strait Pilots, 1877

If in any place near the Torres Strait was settled so as to place buoys and have pilots it certainly would be an expeditious route into the Indian from the Pacific Ocean, but until that is the case, I feel the intricacy of the channel will be a bar to the route being followed.

Phillip Parker King, 1805

In 1877, the government administration, residency and garrison at Somerset were moved to Thursday Island (Waibene), which became the administrative centre for the region. Thursday Island is one of the smallest islands of the Prince of Wales Group, about two miles long and one mile wide, it lies within a protected enclosure provided by its surrounding neighbours: Tuesday, Wednesday, Horn, Prince of Wales, Friday, Goode and Hammond Islands, and is sheltered by them from the buffeting trade winds. The southern side of Thursday Island was selected for the settlement because of its deep-water harbour.

This whole area is essentially tropical and the weather is firmly dictated by the season. In summer, from December to March, the Northwest Monsoon brings hot and humid conditions, occasional storms and heavy downpours. In winter, from April to November, it is dry and dusty with a seemingly interminable southeast wind.

Henry Chester moved from Somerset before Christmas 1877 to be the first Police Magistrate on Thursday Island where he was in residence in a house built on the hill above Hospital Point, with a staff of five water police and access to the Queensland Government vessel *Lizzie Jardine*. Soon, Chester was joined by his wife and, on frequent occasions, entertained officers from visiting ships on the wide veranda of his residency. From there he ruled for eight years, establishing a relatively orderly multinational community with a thriving pearl shell industry whose annual exports were valued at £87,000. Europeans living in the Torres Strait were mostly government-appointed magistrates, customs officers (sometimes with their families), and other people working in the maritime industries or engaged as missionaries. The total Islander population was estimated to be no more than about 3,000 people, plus a transient population of South Sea Islanders, Malays, Filipinos, and Japanese workers employed in the maritime industries.

In 1879, the Queensland Government passed the Queensland Coast Islands Act, which extended the colony's boundary to include almost all the remaining Torres Strait islands to the north and east. The annexation effectively meant that all of the Torres Strait areas came within Queensland borders, giving the Queensland Government control over the marine and other industries, as well as the movement of people between Papua New Guinea, the Torres Strait, and mainland Australia. As a result, the Islanders lost much of their freedom of movement and their traditional culture of self-management. The position of Government Resident was gazetted to formalise administrative control of the Strait and John Douglas (a former Premier of Queensland) was appointed Government Resident and Police Magistrate at Waibene (Thursday Island). His benevolent 'paternalism' ensured an impartial local court and an honest police force, and he reinstated previous measures of local government for the Islanders. In 1900 he proposed that the Islanders should be given full citizenship rights and he wrote:

> They are a civilized people. They marry and are given in marriage; they live in good houses. They are human beings; they are our flesh and blood. They are born under our jurisdiction and they are entitled to the privileges we enjoy. The natives of the Torres Strait are capable of exercising all the rights of British citizens, and they ought to be regarded as such.

Douglas resisted any attempt to bring the Islanders under the Queensland Government's 1879 Act, but following his death in 1904, the term 'Aboriginal' was informally reinterpreted to include Torres Strait Islanders, and they were now aborigines for the purposes of legislation that segregated and controlled Queensland's Indigenous peoples.

Owing to the expansion of the pearl shell industry, the Thursday Island population slowly grew, and by 1885, there were two popular hotels. It developed the nickname of 'Thirsty Island' and the pile of beer bottles outside the rear of the hotels were said to be monumental. It was in the same year that Thursday Island was officially opened for private settlement with forty allotments offered for sale. The settlement grew rapidly, and by 1885, the first census counted that amongst the outsiders, there were 139 Europeans, 77 Malays, 49 Filipinos, 20 Sri Lankans, 16 South Sea Islanders, 7 Japanese, 4 Arabs and 3 Chinese. Visitors to Thursday Island found it to be more like an Asian than an Australian town. There was a collection of Australian seamen who had washed up on Thursday Island, but also South Sea Islanders, Filipino sailors, Japanese divers, barefoot Malays in loose sarongs, Chinese in blue trousers, skull caps and pigtails, Japanese women in kimonos, a Japanese temple, a Chinese 'joss house', and the shops appeared to be mostly controlled by Chinese and Japanese merchants.

The Eastern and Australian Mail Steam Company was registered in London in 1873 and was destined to play an important part in the future steamship trade between the Orient and Australia. The start of this service began in 1874 when the steamship *Sun Foo* left Brisbane bound for Gladstone, Bowen, Cardwell, Somerset, Surabaya, Batavia and Singapore. Guided by the Barrier Reef pilot Captain James Peake, the northbound voyage of the *Sun Foo* was historic because it was the first voyage of the E & A Steam Company and the start of the Barrier Reef and Torres Strait pilot service.

A Pilot station was positioned on Goode Island to service ships passing through the Prince of Wales channel since tides of up to seven or eight knots race backwards and forwards through the channel, which is littered with rocks and reefs. In the narrowest part of the channel, a gap of just over half a mile separates Sunk Reef and Mecca Reef, and the edges of neither are visible.

RMS Somerset arrived at her namesake port in 1874, and in the following years, the ships *Normanby*, *Brisbane*, *Singapore* and *Bowen* joined the service. The first steamer to call into Thursday Island and its new port, Port Kennedy, was the E&A's *RMS Brisbane* in 1878. Soon after, Thursday Island acquired coaling facilities, so steamer visits to Somerset declined and eventually ceased altogether.

RMS Brisbane
Queensland Maritime Association

Subsequently, the British India Navigation Company received a Queensland Government contract in 1880 to provide services all the way from London to Brisbane via India and Batavia. It was the *Merkara* that pioneered the mail service between England and Queensland through the Torres Strait. Another contract was awarded in 1882 to the China Navigation Company, which would sail from Hong Kong via the Torres Strait to Brisbane and Sydney.

As these large commercial steamships began to traverse the Torres Strait it became necessary to have an experienced Torres Strait pilot on board. The pilot knows how the reefs, islands, rocks and shoals appear at all stages of time and tide, and how the currents can change with each passing mile. His knowledge is necessary to pass dangers at close range and to meet and pass other ships in tight areas. As time went on, easily recognised navigation marks such as beacons, buoys and light vessels were established to aid navigation.

In 1884 the 'Regulations for Pilot Service, Torres Strait' were published in the Government Gazette. The regulations covered the issue of licences, licence fees and pilotage fees, penalties for pilotage without a licence and penalties for misconduct. The next step was the issue of five licences to suitably qualified and experienced mariners. Fortunately, the E&A personnel had acquired a working knowledge of the Strait and developed skills in the art of reef pilotage. This group of men were among the first to receive official coast pilot licences and formed the nucleus of a pilot service regulated and licenced by the Marine Board. Thanks to the work of the Royal Navy Hydrographers over many years and the new standards brought to the business of reef pilotage, shipowners could now depend on the safety of defined routes through the Torres Strait and the Inner or Outer Route to the south on what would become the longest single-handed pilotage service in the world. The Prince of Wales channel is now the main route for commercial vessels passing through the Strait but is limited to ships with no more than 12.2 metres of draught and it is required to have a Torres Strait pilot on board to ensure both a safe passage and the protection of the environment.

However, on 28 February 1890, the British India mail steamer *Quetta* bound for London, commanded by Captain Saunders and in the charge of coast pilot Captain Keating, was northbound in the Torres Strait near Albany Island. The dusk gave way to a clear moonlight night; Captain Keating could see Albany Island and the ragged hills of Cape York on his portside and decided he could see well enough to continue onwards into the Adolphus Channel, where the outline of Adolphus Island could be seen against a star-studded sky on his starboard side. A few minutes later, at 9:15 pm, his ship shuddered, heeled, wallowed and then, in three minutes, had sunk. In an area assumed to be clear of obstruction, the *Quetta* hit a sharp pinnacle of coral-encrusted rock, rising to within 15 feet of the surface, which ripped open her starboard side. Startled men, women and children, many of whom had been asleep in their cabins, were washed into the sea.

Amid the confusion, Captain Keating quickly took compass bearings, wrapped his charts in a waterproof bag and then helped to hand out lifebelts to the panic-stricken passengers. As the sea overwhelmed the bridge, he and Captain Saunders were able to reach a lifeboat. Those passengers who could not reach the lifeboats clung desperately to any wreckage that would help keep them afloat. Many drowned, but some were carried by the tide to nearby islands. Survivors and bodies alike drifted all over the Adolphus Channel.

John Jardine's son Frank had returned to reside at Somerset. At daylight, he saw the results of what had happened and sent a message to the telegraph station at Peak Hill twenty-four kilometres to the west. The news was swiftly telegraphed to Thursday Island and Brisbane. A rescue mission was quickly assembled on Thursday Island, and two Government steamers made full speed to the area, followed by several pearling luggers.

The death toll was high, and of the 292 people on board, only 160 survived. One of the survivors was an unknown child, only 18 months old, who was adopted by Captain Edmonson Brown, who lived on Thursday Island. He gave her the name Cissy, but for the rest of her life, she was known as *Quetta*. At the Marine Board inquiry, both

Captain Sanders and the pilot, Captain Keating, were absolved from blame as the rock their ship had struck had been previously unknown and uncharted. Keating even received mild praise:

> The Master exerted himself to the utmost after the vessel struck, whilst the pilot seems to have been very careful and attentive to the navigation of the vessel and the course he steered was the one recommended on the Admiralty Chart corrected to 1887. He appears to have been very cool and collected throughout.

The Quetta disaster had a profound impact on the people of Thursday Island. Reverend McLaren raised 2000 pounds through a public appeal to construct a Memorial Church on the island. As a lasting monument to those who died, the Anglican community named their church, then under construction, the Quetta Memorial Church. Parts of the ship, raised by divers, were incorporated into the workings and furnishing of the church. These included the ship's bell, a compass bowl, a riding lamp and some timbers made into pews. Other relics from the ship – a porthole, a lifebuoy and a flag are on permanent display, and the entire church is a poignant reminder of the perils at sea.

The Quetta tragedy did not mark the end of maritime disasters in the Torres Strait, but charts of the area were continually being updated and improved. Lights and beacons were gradually increasing in number along the Strait, and the expansion of steamer traffic led, in turn, to the continued development of the pilot service by experienced former shipmasters with extensive local knowledge.

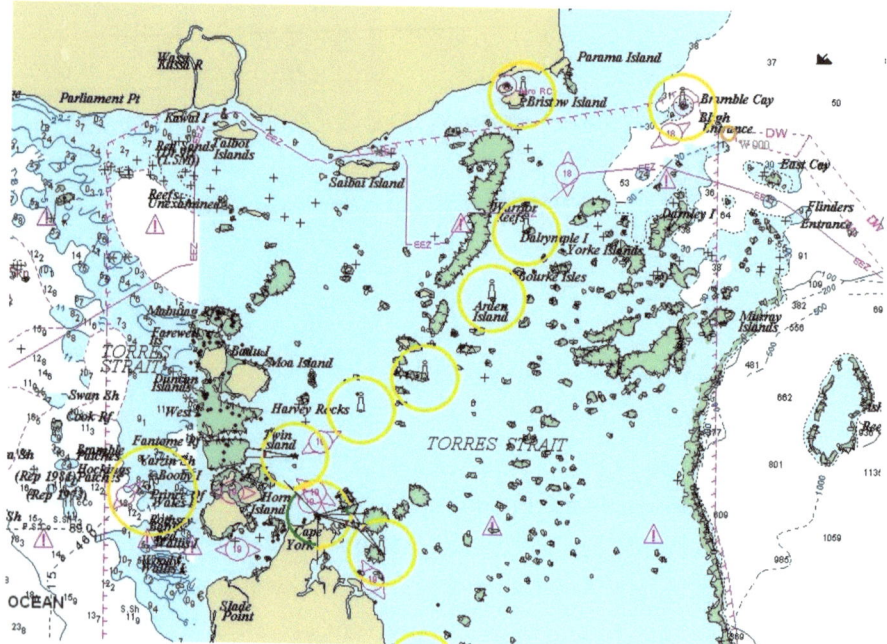

Torres Strait Marine Chart showing navigational markers along the main shipping channels

Epilogue

The voyages of the early explorers such as Torres, Cook, Bligh, and Flinders first found a way through this reef-strewn passage. The British Naval hydrographers such as King, Wickham, Blackwood, Yule and Stanley contributed to charting the Torres Strait and defined the Bligh Entrance, the Great Northeast Channel and the Prince of Wales Channel as the safest route. Finally, it was the work of the Torres Strait pilots and the placing of navigational markers that ultimately led to the use of this dangerous passage as a major shipping route.

At the beginning of the twentieth century Thursday Island had become the centre of a flourishing maritime industry, with a hospital, artillery battery, post office, schools and four pubs.

Over time, the skills of Torres Strait Islanders, their conversion to Christianity, intermarriage with South Sea Islanders and adoption of their customs differentiated them from both neighbouring Papuan and Aboriginal peoples. Despite Alfred Haddon's prediction that modernity would destroy the underlying fabric of Islander identity, family and kin relationships and a deep sense of belonging to place remain at the heart of Islander culture.

Horn Island airport has a dramatic history, as it was an important staging base for Allied air missions against the Japanese and a stop-over for fighter aircraft heading to New Guinea. From March 1942 until June 1943, eight Japanese bombing raids were made on the Horn Island airfield, which became the only military installation in Queensland to be regularly targeted by the Japanese military.

Migration to mainland Australia developed after the Second World War. The 2011 Census showed the number of people who identified as Torres Strait Islanders and who live in the Torres Strait or on Cape York at Bamaga and Seisia as 8,738. The same census showed the number of people who identified as Torres Strait Islanders and who live on the mainland as 38,134.

Commercial fishing is one of the most economically important activities in the Torres Strait and provides a significant opportunity for financial independence for the region's traditional inhabitants. The commercial fisheries include prawn, tropical rock lobster, Spanish mackerel, pearl shell, barramundi, fin fish, crab, trochus, and sea cucumber in order of value. The Protected Zone Joint Authority (PZJA) was established in 1984 and has a policy of maximising the opportunities for Islander participation in all sectors of the commercial fishing industry. There has been a buy-back of previous licences, and new licences are restricted to traditional inhabitants. Rock lobsters are usually collected by small family units, employing an aluminium dinghy, outboard motor, and hookah diving gear. It provides opportunities for local entrepreneurs, with a bag limit of three per person or six per boat.

Before the Endeavour left England in 1768, Lord Morton, the President of the Royal Society, had provided Cook and Banks with suggestions on how to conduct themselves during encounters with local inhabitants and strongly argued for the upholding of the indigenous people's land rights. Regretfully, this defence of indigenous land rights was forgotten in subsequent years of colonial occupation.

Eddie Koiki Mabo was born on the island of Mer on June 1936. He was an activist throughout his life, campaigning for workers' rights, indigenous education and land rights for indigenous people. In August 1981, he gave a speech at a conference at James Cook University in Townsville outlining the history of traditional land ownership on Mer. Following the conference, a group of Murray Islanders decided to launch a land rights claim, and in 1982, a statement of claim was filed in the High Court of Australia. Launching a legal challenge required considerable research to substantiate the land claim. The Murray Islanders assembled anthropological reports and drawings of the island showing family property boundaries, annotated with natural identifiers such as a Wongai tree and a Kozo tree. The drawings were supported by photographs showing the location of boundary markers on the island. The facts of the case were debated in several court cases, first in the Supreme Court of Queensland and then in the High Court of Australia.

It would be a decade before the case was finally resolved when the High Court of Australia delivered its decision in 1992. In the Mabo decision, the High Court recognised the land rights of the Meriam people, traditional owners of the Murray Islands (Mer, Dauer, and Waier) in the Torres Strait and that the people of Mer were 'entitled as against the whole world to possession, occupation, use and enjoyment of the lands of the Murray Islands'.

In this decision, the High Court also ruled that the lands of the Australian continent were not *terra nullus* or 'land belonging to no one' when European settlement occurred. This was one of the most significant legal decisions ever made in Australia, and it granted the recognition of native title across all of Australia. Eddie Mabo's attempt to regain title to his garden plot on the island of Mer changed the course of history, and it was the island mode of horticulture that helped unpick White Australia's creation myth of a *terra nullus*.

Bibliography

Babbage, Ross The Strategic Significance of Torres Strait Canberra Papers on Strategy and Defence Canberra 1990

Beete, Jukes A Narrative of the surveying voyage of the HMS Fly, 2 Volumes Cambridge University Press Cambridge 1847

Bligh, William Bligh's Voyage to the South Seas in HM Ship Bounty Project Gutenberg 2005

Bligh, William A Narrative of the Mutiny on the Bounty Project Gutenberg 2007

Burnet, Ian The Tasman Map Rosenberg Publishing Sydney 2019

Burnet, Ian Archipelago Rosenberg Publishing Sydney 2015

Cane, Scott First Footprints Allen and Unwin Sydney 2013

Causer, Tim Memorandoms by James Martin UCL Press London 2017

Dampier, William A New Voyage Around the World John Carter Brown Library 1699

Dampier, William A Voyage to New Holland in the Year 1699 Project Gutenberg London 1729

Davis, Richard Woven Histories, Dancing Lives Aboriginal Studies Press Canberra 2004

Dooley, Gillian Mathew Flinders: The Man behind the Map Wakefield Press Adelaide 2022

Flannery, Tim Terra Australis Text Publishing Melbourne 2000

Flinders, Mathew A Voyage to Terra Australis Volume 1 G and W Nichol London 1814

Flinders, Mathew A Voyage to Terra Australis Volume 2 G and W Nichol London 1814

Foley, John Reef Pilots Banks Bros and Street Sydney 1982

Foley, John Timeless Isle Torres Strait Historical Society Thursday Island 1982

Fornasiero, Jean Encountering Terra Australis Wakefield Press Kent Town 2004

Gesner, Peter Memoirs of the Queensland Museum - The Pandora Project Queensland Museum Brisbane 2016

Haddon, A.C. Cambridge Anthropological Expedition to the Torres Strait, Volume 1-5 Cambridge University Press Cambridge 1912

Hamilton, George A Voyage around the World in HM Frigate Pandora Horden House Sydney 1998

Hilder, Brett The Voyage of Torres University of Queensland Press Brisbane 1976

Hirst, Warwick Wreck: The Fatal Voyage of the Charles Eaton Inspiring Publishers Canberra 2015

Horden, Marsden King of the Australian Coast Miegunyah Press Melbourne 1997

Hordern, Miles Passage to Torres Strait John Murray London 2005

Horsburgh, James Directions for sailing to and from the East Indies, China and Australia William Allen and Company London 1841-43

Ireland, John The Shipwrecked Orphans Babcock New Haven 1845

King, Phillip Parker Narrative of a Survey of the Coasts of Australia, 1818-1822 Volume 1 John Murray London 1825

Lee, Ida Captain Bligh's Second Voyage to the South Sea Longmans, Green and Company London 1920

Macmillan, David A Squatter went to Sea Currawong Publishing Sydney 1957

Nicholson Ian Via Torres Strait The Roebuck Society Nambour 1996

Parkin, Ray Endeavour Meigunya Melbourne 2020

Peak, Veronica Charles Eaton: Wake for the Melancholy Shipwreck www.veronicapeak.com

Prado, Don Diego Relacion Summaria de Capitan Don Diego de Prado State Library NSW Sydney

Rosenman, Helen Two Voyages to the South Seas University of Hawaii Press Honolulu 1998

Scott, Ernest The Life of Captain Mathew Flinders Angus and Robertson Sydney 1914

Singe, John The Torres Strait University of Queensland Press Brisbane 1979

Tench, Watkin A Narrative of the expedition to Botany Bay Project Gutenberg 2006

Tench, Watkin A Complete Account of the Settlement at Botany Bay Nicol and Sewell London 1793

Tobin, George Captain Bligh's Second Chance UNSW Press Sydney 2007

Tilley, Robert The Mermaid Tree ABC Books Sydney 200

Other Books

THE TASMAN MAP - Ian Burnet

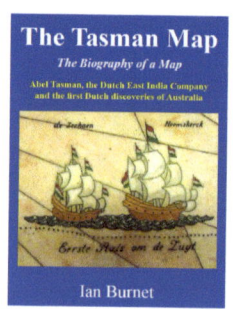

Abel Tasman, the Dutch East India Company and the first Dutch discoveries of Australia

This story of the first Dutch voyages to discover Australia is set against the background of the struggle of the newly formed Dutch Republic to gain its independence from the Kingdom of Spain and the struggle of the Dutch East India Company for trade supremacy in the East Indies against its Portuguese, Spanish and English rivals. Over a period of only forty years from 1606 to 1644 and based on sixteen separate discoveries the first map of Australia took shape. The Tasman Map shows a recognizable outline of the north, west and south coasts of Australia that was not to change for another 125 years until the British explorer James Cook charted the east coast in 1770.

It was in 1925 and 1933 that the Mitchell Library in Sydney, Australia, acquired both the Tasman Huydecoper Journal and the Tasman Bonaparte Map. The story of how the library managed to acquire these treasures of Dutch exploration and cartography will bring new recognition to these icons of both Dutch and Australian history.

ISBN 9780645106848 paperback $39.99
Ebook ISBN 9780645106831 $19.95

JOSEPH CONRAD'S EASTERN VOYAGES - Ian Burnet
Tales of Singapore and an East Borneo River

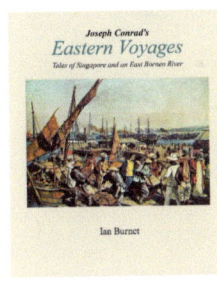

The life of Józef Teodor Konrad Korzeniowski reads like an adventure story, an adventure story that could be written by somebody like Joseph Conrad. The young Conrad dreamed of a life at sea, he eventually became a British merchant seaman and he spent fifteen years sailing on the classic three-masted, square-rigged sailing clippers before they were ultimately replaced by steamships. During this period he worked his way up from apprentice, to third mate, to second mate, to first mate and finally the captain of one of these beautiful ships.

Joseph Conrad once said that everything about his life can be found in his books. Because the material for his first books are mainly autobiographical then Ian Burnet has been able to use a mixture of his own words, together with those of Conrad, to tell this story of Joseph Conrad's eastern voyages and his tales of Singapore and an East Borneo River.

Conrad loved the 'mysterious East' and his first books – *Almayers Folly*, *An Outcast of the Islands*, *Lord Jim* and *The Rescue* were all set in Borneo and based on the people and places he encountered in his own voyages as first mate on a trading vessel based out of Singapore. In this book Ian Burnet connects the fictional and real worlds of Conrad's life in Southeast Asia.

ISBN 9780645106800 paperback $34.99
Ebook ISBN 9780645106817 $19.95

www.ingramcontent.com/pod-product-compliance
Lightning Source LLC
Chambersburg PA
CBHW042042290426
44109CB00001B/4